World Famous CEOs and their Business Mantras

Publishers
Pustak Mahal®

Administrative office and sale centre
J-3/16 , Daryaganj, New Delhi-110002
☎ 011-23276539, 23272783, 23272784, 23260518
E-mail: info@pustakmahal.com • *Website:* www.pustakmahal.com

Branches
Bengaluru: ☎ 080-22234025, 080-40912845
E-mail: pustakmahalblr@gmail.com
Mumbai: ☎ 022-22010941, 022-22053387
E-mail: unicornbooksmumbai@gmail.com

ISBN 978-81-223-1322-2

Edition: 2019

Printed at : *Radha Offset, Delhi*

Contents

Introduction

This book is dedicated to fifty-four entrepreneurs who have made a difference in their relevant industries, and radically changed the way companies presently do business. They forever changed the landscape with innovative methods of doing business, unique and keen senses of how things should be, and by daring to go against the grain. To them, thinking outside the box was a normal thought process, and then implementing those ideals was only common sense. Consequently, billionaires were made because of their astute observations.

Whether these men and women controlled the helm of existing corporations, instrumental in making a difference to the profitability of the companies, or they started their own companies, growing them to well-known conglomerates, each man and woman had the same drive and tenacity that made him a famous CEO. Most were ambitious as children, and sought to break out of the mold in which they were raised. Some were geniuses as children and excelled at an early age. Others were not necessarily overly-smart, but were, nonetheless, ambitious and zealous in their pursuits. And, although all of them come from a variety of backgrounds, both rich and poor, they have similar traits that make them great entrepreneurs and leaders.

Famous CEOs can rise to stardom through controversial means, or by plain-old-good business acumen. We have chosen to focus our discussion on the latter. Anyone can become an instant hit by doing something underhanded. But, for the fifty-four men and women that we have chosen, they met the ultimate challenge. They decided to make something of themselves, and have left indelible marks in both the business world and the companies they led. They were inspirations and money makers. Business excellence is how they are remembered.

The most important reason for these men and women to be on the famous CEOs is because they changed history. They all have defining moments that made the business community and general public stand up and say "wow". Some now have their own schools, others possessed philosophies that are taught at schools around the world. Some believe that their wealth should be dispersed and better done so while they are alive to make a difference. And, even though many of these men are retired, they still contribute to society in a meaningful way.

What is most interesting is that despite the fact that all of these fifty-four men and women had the ability to complete a university education, not all of them did, preferring to drop out and jump right into their endeavours. Another commonality is that none of them stood up and said that they would be great some day. They never said their goals were to be rich and famous. They focused on the process that made them happy, or the development of something that they knew should have validity. They formulated their ideals and pushed them forward to create tangible enterprises, and services or products of the future. And, as each man did so, he was not necessarily saying that he was awesome. He just knew there was a better way, and he had identified it.

World Famous CEOs and their Business Mantra's is a positive and interesting look at the profiles of men and women who made a difference, and how they accomplished those defining moments.

Adrian Gore

Founder and CEO,
Discovery Holdings Ltd.

Now one of the best-known businessmen in South Africa, Gore is the CEO and founder of Discovery Holdings, a major player in the international health and life assurance markets. It now encompasses Discovery Health, Vitality and Discovery Life in South Africa, Prudential Health in the UK and Destiny Health in the US. Described by some as obsessive, Gore has an ability to think outside the box that has earned Discovery a reputation for innovative products. Under his guidance, membership has grown to nearly 2 million.

Biography:

Born in Johannesburg, South Africa, in 1964, Gore graduated from the University of the Witwatersrand, Johannesburg, with a BSc (Hons) in Actual Science. In 1990, he was admitted as a Fellow of the Faculty of Actuaries (Edinburgh, Scotland) and in 1992 as an Associate of the Society of Actuaries (Chicago).

Picking a Gap in the Market:

Helping out with his father's tobacco and confectionery business convinced Gore that a career in retail was not for him. After a degree in Actuarial Science, he joined Liberty Life as an actuary and helped develop its Medical Lifestyle product. However, it was a period of economic uncertainty, and as industry costs began to rise, Gore spotted the potential for a medical scheme that offered sustainability. Coupled with the desire to create his own business, Gore founded Discovery Holdings Ltd.

Believing in Innovation:

Since its inception, Discovery has made innovation its keyword, and Gore believes this is crucial to survival. However, he is disciplined about introducing new products, being careful not to innovate for innovation's sake. After starting out in the healthcare insurance industry, Gore led Discovery to become a pioneer in the life insurance market.

In 2001, he launched a product that was 20 per cent cheaper than its competitors, by taking out the unnecessary investment part of the insurance. Within months, the rest of the market did the same and life insurance cost declined across the industry. Displaying the strategic vision for which he had become known Gore turned to preventative health measures, launching the Vitality loyalty and wellness programme, for which the company holds a worldwide patent.

When rapid growth threatened to affect operational efficiency, Gore restructured the call centre, leading to an instant improvement in service. His personality and self-belief have attracted some of South Africa's brightest personnel, giving Discovery a vital edge.

Leadership Style:

Astute, competitive, consensual. Renowned for his tenacity and drive, Gore has little patience for laziness or wasted time.

Business Lessons:

Gore has always believed it is important to have what he calls a "noble cause and purpose" in business. It is better to be motivated by progress, change and innovation than money. A CEO does not get up in the morning thinking about money.

- Join a company whose objectives you identify with and whose success you can enjoy and feel proud of.

- In a new role, make sure you are seen to be looking at a career rather than today's take-home pay.
- Define a personal and business vision that makes you look forward to going to work.

Key Strength:

A brilliant strategist and problem-solver, Gore is the ultimate optimist.

Best Decision:

Forming his own company at the age of 28.

Alan George Lafley

Former Chairman and CEO, Procter and Gamble

Procter & Gamble, the world's biggest consumer-products company, was in crisis when A.G. Lafley took over the top job in 2000. Eighteen months earlier, concern about the need for change had led to the appointment as CEO of Durk Jager, whose attempts at a rapid shake-up left the company in turmoil and triggered a boardroom coup. Lafley was chosen to restore equilibrium, which he did, but he also brought about a quiet revolution in the culture and the marketing strategy of this bastion of corporate conservatism.

Biography:

Born in New Hampshire in 1947, the son of a General Electric executive, Lafley graduated from Hamilton College in 1969. He began a doctorate in medieval and renaissance history at the University of Virginia, but left to spend five years in the US Navy. He enrolled in Harvard's MBA programme in 1975.

Company Man:

Procter & Gamble (P&G) is known as an insider's company, and Lafley was the classic company man. He joined in 1977 as a brand assistant for Joy dish detergent. He worked his way up through the ranks to become president of Global Beauty Care and P&G North America. When he was drafted to take over after Jager, it was his reputation as a steady, calming influence that had put him at the top of the list. As it turned out, his enthusiastic, mild-mannered approach proved capable of changing more than any aggression had.

Quiet Revolutionary:

Lafley's gentle style masked a firm decisiveness and a long-thought-out set of ideas about how to make P&G relevant in the 21st century, when speed and agility would be far more important than sheer size. In his quiet way, Lafley led the most sweeping transformation of the company since its foundation in 1837. Lafley pushed through the largest acquisitions in its history, at the same time replacing over half of the top tier of executies, more than any P&G boss in memory, and cutting nearly 10,000 jobs. Lafley also moved more women into senior positions.

He nailed firmly into place the central tenet of his vision: that P&G should do what it does best – selling solid, reliable, major brands such as Tide, Pampers and Crest – and nothing else. He also made it clear that the company's stodgy corporate culture, the very problem that had triggered his predecessor's zealous rush for change, was gone forever.

Lafley achieved these profound changes by listening, asking and quietly explaining – proving that, if your ideas are good enough, there's no need to shout.

Leadership Style:

As an expert delegator, Lafley shaped decisions by asking keen questions, and made nurturing talent one of his highest priorities. He forbade long meetings, hated PowerPoint displays, and encouraged executives to discuss rather than just present point of view.

Business Lessons:

Instead of always trying to develop the Next Big Thing, focus on what you do best and make sure you keep doing it better. Improving what you do can be more successful than changing everything.

- If it's not broken don't fix it; stick to your knitting – that is, improve what you do now.

- Bring out new products when you need to but make sure key customers will welcome them.
- Introduce new products into existing markets, or take old products into new markets. Beware starting a new market with a new product.

Key Strength:

Using stability and focusing on a considered strategy to create change.

Best Decision:

Telling his managers to focus on what they did well. This formed the basis for radical change.

Amancio Ortega Gaona

Chairman, Inditex

The richest man in Spain and at one time the eighth richest in the world, with a fortune of $20 billion, Ortega is a self-made success. Building the Zara fashion retail chain from nothing, it now has 3,000 branches in 64 countries. His story is one of hard work, opportunism, and skilled market analysis. Ortega has bucked market trends consistently, always doing things differently to give his shops a unique appeal. His company produces a large range of designs in small numbers, which keeps his customers interested and coming back for more.

Biography:

Born in 1936 in Leon, Spain. Ortega dropped out to school, and had no formal higher education.

Looks Similar, Costs Less:

Living in the centre of the Iberian textile industry, La Coruna, Ortega entered the business aged 14 and in his twenties he was making bathrobes and lingerie in his living room. In the 1960s Ortega realized that it was not only wealthy people who appreciated expensive, well-designed clothes, and he came up with the simple idea of using cheaper fabrics to produce similar-looking items at prices that everyone could afford. In the mid 1970s he opened his first Zara store.

Fast Fashion Innovator:

Zara is still principally known for the same thing – expensive-looking, trendy clothes at reasonable prices – but it is the unique way Ortega has found to deliver this in a highly competitive market that best reflects his talent. Aware that costs mounted and time was lost as garments moved from designers to factories to stores, he saw the importance of delivering direct to customers.

The business strategy he has developed involves controlling all aspects of the chain, reducing costs and gaining speed and thereby flexibility. His designers get ideas from fashion shows and respond quickly to trends. Keeping manufacture in Spain, rather than following the trend of outsourcing to countries with lower labour costs, speeds up his operation – the clothes are designed and in-store within weeks. Stores are freshly stocked twice a week, avoiding high inventory cost and clearout sales, and encouraging customers to visit often.

The highly successful flotation of his holding company Inditex – which also owns Massimo Dutti and Pull and Bear – in 2001 has had little effect on his unpretentious lifestyle.

Leadership Style:

Hands-on, low profile, and relaxed. His ego-free style is said to be key to his success. He himself wears jeans and no tie, and he lives modestly in his home city of La Coruna.

Business Lessons:

There is no need to cultivate a celebrity cheif executive status when you have a strong product and a good strategy. Ortega has never given an interview and has allowed few pictures of him to be made public.

- Ask yourself if you are seeking publicity to advance your company or to put yourself in the spotlight.
- Remember that, with few exceptions, CEOs eventually hit big problems. Don't make them more public than you need.

• The top jobs are listening jobs; avoid making yourself the key to the brand and big up your team instead.

Key Strength:

Innovation. Ortega understands how to make his stores constantly interesting, enticing customers to return frequently and promote sales through word of mouth.

Best Decision:

Resisting the temptation to outsource manufacturing, prizing flexibility and speed above low production costs.

Andy Grove

President, Chairman and CEO (1987-98), Intel Corp.

Born Andras Istvan Grof, Grove fled the Soviet invasion of Hungary in 1956 to become one of the corporate America's most successful and best-known CEOs. A gifted and entirely self-taught manager, Grove provided the strategic savvy and business brains to match the technical expertise of his fellow Intel co-founders Gordon Moore and Robert Noyce. Under Grove's stewardship, Intel underwent drastic restructuring to become the first high-tech giant of the silicon era, and for a time the world's most valuable company.

Biography:

Born in Budapest in 1936. After the 1956 Soviet invasion of Hungary, Grove left his home and family to emigrate to the US. In 2000, Grove was diagnosed with Parkinson's disease.

Corporate Visionary:

As part of the founding team, and as President from 1979, Grove helped to create a vastly successful company from Intel's famous memory chips. But with Intel flying high, it was his seminal restructuring of the business the elevated him to the status of genuine business legend. Spotting what he would later call a "strategic inflection point", Grove decided in the early 1980s to abandon the lucrative computer memory chip trade that Intel had dominated for 20 years in favour of the risky new business of microprocessor manufacture.

It was an extraordinary and controversial decision, almost as if Coca-Cola were abandoning fizzy drinks or Ford had decided to make bicycles rather than cars, but he was right. Within a few short years, the price of memory had collapsed as Japanese competition boomed, while the success of the IBM PC meant that Intel was sitting on top of yet another vast fortune as the biggest supplier of microprocessors in the world. Grove wrote a best-selling book about the experience, which remains one of the most memorable titles of all business homes: Only the Paranoid Survive.

Productivity Powerhouse:

Famous for his unflinchingly direct approach and love of argument, Grove's Intel may not always have been a fun place to work, but it was extraordinary productive. He was a pioneer of Management by Objective: measuring, recording, and managing every detail of every employee's personal productivity. He also insisted on forensic dissections of the reasons behind the firm's occasional failures, in order nerve to make the same mistake twice.

Leadership Style:

Constructive confrontation. Famous for shouting down ideas he didn't like and for shutting latecomers out of meetings, Grove could also be charming, generous, and supportive.

Business Lessons:

The most successful companies seek constantly to reinvent themselves if they are to keep ahead of the competition. The pace at which Intel operated was punishing, and employee turnover could be high as a consequence, but Grove drove himself and he got results.

- Promote people who welcome a fast pace of change; given more responsibility they may blossom.
- Put systems that give managers the information they need in time to make rapid decisions.
- Some people do not fit into an environment of continuous change; if they are reluctant move them out.

Key Strength:

Grove had the rare ability to put himself outside the pressures of both the organization and the moment, and to see situations from a dispassionate perspective.

Best Decision:

Reinventing the company as a manufacturer of microprocessors instead of memory chips.

Anil Ambani

CEO, Reliance ADA

The financial "whiz kid" of the company, Ambani is the chairman of Reliance Capital and Reliance Communications, chairman and managing director of Reliance Energy, and was formerly vice chairman and MD of Reliance Industries Ltd. He and his estranged brother Mukesh enjoy wealth that places them among the top ten richest people in the world, and their rival Reliance empires dominate the Indian economy. Anil Ambani holds one of the world's fastest-growing dollar fortunes.

Biography:

Born in Bombay (Mumbai), India, in 1959. The son of entrepreneur Dhirubhai Ambani. He spent his early years in a Bombay slum where seven members of the family lived in one room, while his father strove to build his business interests. Ambani holds a BSc from the University of Bombay and an MBA from The Wharton School at the University of Pennsylvania.

Learning Curve:

From an early age, the Ambani brothers were given ambitious goals. When Anil returned from Wharton Business School in 1982, the day after completing his master degree in 14 months instead of 24, he thought he was due a break. His father had other ideas: that evening he was dispatched to the company's textile plant in Ahmadabad, where he spent the next five years learning the business from the ground up.

Within Reliance, Anil is the Ambani with the head for figures. As co-CEO in the 80s, he is credited with many financial innovations in the Indian capital markets.

A Bollywood Ending?

The Ambanis were only in their twenties when their father had a stroke, forcing them to take control of the company. Anil says this time was the toughest but most valuable period of his life. The brothers agreed on a process of backward integration from the manufacture of polyester cloth to petrochemicals and oil refining.

Following the death of their father, tensions between the brothers came to a head in late 2005, when a long-simmering disagreement over company strategy erupted into a highly publicized feud. In the end, a truce was brokered by his mother, Kokilaben, and the Reliance Empire was broken up in 2006 with Anil controlling the telecommunications, energy and capital finance interests.

Since 2005, when he took over Indian film production and distribution company Ad labs, Ambani has had interests in the entertainment industry. His current projects include the creation of one of the world's largest entertainment conglomerates.

Leadership Style:

Driven, focused, and willing to listen to criticism. Ambani once embarked on a fitness regime when a colleague pointed out that if he was out of shape, his company was also likely to be out of shape.

Business Lessons:

Many of Ambani's business principles were learned at his father's knee. One of the key lessons was the importance of earning the respect of the people who work for him.

- Talk to every person you come across in your organization, from a cleaner to your main shareholder.
- Gain trust from your stakeholders by never letting anyone down – avoid defaulting on any promise.

- Make sure all your people understand that they all have an important role in your organization. By creating an atmosphere of respect for each other's contributions, you will gain respect in turn.

Key Strength:

An extremely competitive streak and a keen eye for investment. Described as having a killer instinct, he has been referred to as the Indian Warren Buffett.

Best Decision:

Taking full responsibility for his role in the family business after his father suffered a stroke.

Ashok Khosla

President, International Union for Conservation of Nature

A leading expert on the environment and sustainable development, Khosla was appointed head of the world's oldest and largest global environmental network in late 2008. He has been involved in a range of initiatives aimed at understanding and utilizing the connections between economic development and the environment for more than 40 years, and he founded a network in India that, over the last quater of a century, has initiated a vast array of schemes to promote development among the country's poor, and improve the environment.

Biography:

Born in Kashmir in 1940, Khosla is the son of a university professor and a college lecturer. He gained a master's degree in natural sciences from Cambridge University, UK and a PhD in experimental physics from Harvard University.

Harvard Pioneer:

In the early 1960s, Khosla helped to design and teach Harvard's first undergraduate course on the environment, which explored the complex interactions between the environment and economic systems, human populations and natural resources. After returning to India in 1972, he became founding director of the government's Office of Environmental Planning and Coordination, the first national environmental agency in a developing country, introducing systems to integrate environmental considerations into the development process.

Model for Sustainability:

In 1983, Khosla founded the sustainable development network-Development Alternatives Groups. It has come to be widely recognized as a leading innovator in using environmentally friendly technologies to create sustainable livelihoods, and enabling local enterprises to meet the needs of rural and low-income communities.

Among its achievements has been the provision of low-cost housing, the creation of more than 300,000 sustainable jobs, the installation of decentralized power stations using renewable fuel, and the reclamation of degraded land through reforestation, watershed management, and ground water restoration.

The broad approach taken by development Alternatives, and the impact it has had, have turned Khosla into one of the best-regarded and most influential figures in the area of environment and sustainable economies. In 2002, he was awarded the UN Environment Prize for creating sustainable livelihoods for people living below the poverty line.

Leadership Style:

A highly inspiring figure, Khosla motivates those around him by demonstrating commitment, and with his broad-based approach to the issues he deals with.

Business Lessons:

Considering the needs of the environment and local people, as well as commercial questions, can be a powerful driver of innovation. Khosla used this message to make energy firms think about their environmental impact.

- CSR should be a major factor in your company's operation, not a self-promoting afterthought. Give back to the communities you work with.
- Give the issue of environmental care to a designated person or department in your organization.

• Inform current and future customers of what you are doing in the area of energy saving.

Key Strength:

Recognizing that sustainability can only come from considering both the economy and the environment.

Best Decision:

Setting up Development Alternatives Group, which created a ground-breaking model for sustainable development.

Bill Gates

Chairman and
CEO (1976-2000),
Microsoft Corp

A floppy, Geeky Appearance and a commitment to large-scale philanthropy may give the impression that Gates is the easygoing type, but you don't become the richest man on earth by being gentle. A confrontational manager and an aggressive business operator, Gates broke the mould of the computer nerd. His ability to play business hardball ensured that his company cashed in from the very beginning of the IT boom, and his demanding managerial presence has kept Microsoft at the heart of the computing world ever since.

Biography:

Born in Seattle in 1955. Gates wrote his first program, a version of noughts and crosses, on a school computer. He enrolled at Harvard in 1973, but left to concentrate on his software business.

College Drop-Out:

After selling a computer program to his school at the age of 17, Gates continued developing software during a brief stint at Harvard. Dropping out of college to concentrate on his IT start-up business, he began creating software for a variety of systems, writing code himself, reviewing every single piece of code the company produced, and keeping an eye out for growth opportunities. When he was offered an agreement to provide the operating system for IBM's new PC in 1980, he saw his big chance.

Aggression and Drive:

Gate's deal with IBM demonstrated his acute business acumen and his taste for tough dealing. As well as providing the operating system for IBM's ubiquitous PCs, Gates insisted that Microsoft retain the copyright to the system, in the hope that he would be able to license it to order hardware manufactures. This contractual masterstroke spawned an entire industry of PCs that all depended on MS-DOS and put Microsoft at the centre of the computing revolution. That one move provided the basis for Microsoft's phenomenal growth.

Gates insisted on the creation of new products to consolidate the company's position, and his aggressive management style continued to drive the business forward. He appointed equally tough partners, such as Steve Ballmer, but also generated a motivating corporate spirit that kept the best people coming to Microsoft. He was even harder on the competition, doing whatever it look to defend Microsoft's dominance. Since 2006, Gates has devoted an increasing proportion of his time to the charitable Bill & Melinda Gates Foundation.

Leadership Style:

Confrontational, direct and abrasive. Gates became renowned for his demanding approach. He also ensured that Microsoft was a meritocracy, that it was product-centred and that it looked after its people.

Business Lessons:

Gates's determination is legendary. Most senior managers know that they may have to choose between being well-liked and less successful or well-respected and capable of developing companies with dominant positions.

- Be prepared to take any steps that will improve your market domination – including litigation.
- Accept that your true aim is to be as near to a monopoly as you can and the law allows.

- When you've established a dominant position, pull out all the stops to defend it. Keep pushing or your dominance will crumble.

Key Strength:

Looking for improvement, always and everywhere.

Best Decision:

Insisting on keeping the copyright to MS-DOS in the 1980 deal with IBM. This was the key to Microsoft's success.

Brian Goldner

President and CEO,
Hasbro, Inc.

Toy making giant Hasbro was casting around for ways to make the most of its impressive portfolio of classic brands when Goldner became part of its leadership team. Despite its renowned and familiar assets, the company behind Monopoly, G.I. Joe and Mr. Potato Head was having trouble making them count in the new world of technology and entertainment. Goldner's move to turn Transformers and G.I. Joe into movies revolutionized the company, its prospects, and the business model for the toy industry worldwide.

Biography:

Born in Huntington, New York in 1964. Goldner graduated in government at Dartmouth College, New Hampshire, where he was also a radio D.J.

Marketing Talent:

Goldner began his career as a marketing assistant for a health care consulting firm, before moving through jobs at top advertising agencies Leo Burnett and J. Walter Thompson, promoting a broad range of consumer products. By the age of 34, he was a senior partner in JWT's Los Angeles office. One of his tasks was promoting Power Rangers, licensed by Japanese toymaker Bandai, which brought him to the attention of Hasbro.

New Platform:

Goldner moved to Hasbro in 2000, when the venerable US toy and games giant was going through a painful restructure in response to changing leisure habits. Taking charge of the entire US toy division and brands just months into his new job, Goldner returned the company's focus to its own portfolio of toys and games, and began looking for innovative ways to develop them.

After spells as president of US Toys and then COO of Hasbro, Inc., he became CEO in 2008, by which time he had laid the foundations of a major comeback. His most inspired move was approaching film producer Lorenzo di Bonaventura in 2003, after reading that he was interested in making a film about military technology. The producer took up Goldner's suggestion of basing the film on the action toy G.I. Joe, and the contact also led to the film Transformers, which took more that $700 million and triggered the sequel.

Goldner had transformed Hasbro from a toymaker into an intellectual-property-owning powerhouse. As CEO, he has built on this by signing further film deals with Universal Pictures, working with Nintendo on Hasbro based interactive games, and expanding into emerging markets such as Brazil.

Leadership Style:

Goldner takes a team-oriented approach, surrounding himself with people who know things that he doesn't.

Business Lessons:

Bringing an old asset to a new platform and exploiting your intellectual property with another company can bring remarkable results. Since costs will mostly be met by your partner, you can achieve a very high return.

- Study your current market and think broadly about their wants in the future, however unrelated those wants may seem to your current products.

- Look for innovative joint ventures with companies working in the same, or related, markets.
- Study the "width" of your brand – ask yourself how you can expand the types of product the brand sells.

Key Strength:

The breadth of vision to see the possibilities of regenerating Hasbro's classic and familiar brands in new platforms.

Best Decision:

Forging contacts with the film industry, which has turned out to be a lucrative business move.

Charles Ergen

President and CEO, DISH Network & EchoStar

An inspirational story of starting with nothing, spotting a market and going for broke, while outsmarting major players along the way, has characterized Ergen's career. Co-founding cable box and satellite infrastructure company Echosphere (renamed EchoStar) in 1980, and satellite TV subsidiary DISH Network in 1996, put him in the top 100 richest people in the world, with a net worth of almost $10 billion. DISH Network is now the third largest direct-to-home satellite television company in the US, with some 14 million customers.

Biography:

Born in Oak Ridge, Tennessee, in 1953. Ergen graduated from the University of Tennessee with a bachelor's in general business and accounting, and gained an MBA from the Babcock Graduate School of Management at Wake Forest University.

A Gamble That Paid Off:

Ergen's success was built on friendship and an eye for opportunity. Having spotted their first satellite dish in 1980 on a gambling trip to Las Vegas, Ergen and his friend, Jim DeFranco, identified an exciting new market in rural Colorado, where TV reception was poor. Pooling their resources, Ergen his future wife, and DeFranco started a business called Echosphere, selling dishes off the back of a track. The business took off and Ergen's enthusiasm for new technology kept him ahead of his competitors.

An Unconventional Approach:

Ergen bought into the satellite business and in 1992, EchoStar had launched three satellites and registered its millionth customer by 1997. Ergen's technological nous is easily equalled by his business instinct. His sometimes unconventional approach has seen him fearlessly take on far large competitors. In one case he famously distributed free satellite dishes to the whole of Boulder, Colorado, to woo customers away from a rival. He was also the first to sell satellite receivers for under $200. In 1998, he sued Rupert Murdoch's redoubtable News Corporation after Murdosh had withdrawn from a planned merger.

Ergen has also suffered his fair share of misfortunes. In 2008, EchoStar lost one satellite on launch and another through failure. Then Forbes.com reported a 25 per cent drop in DISH Network's shares, following its split from EchoStar, and EchoStar paid out $105 million in compensation to TiVo, Inc. over a patent breach. Observers believe it is only a question of time before Ergen bounces back.

Leadership Style:

Aggressive, opportunistic, focused. Ergen is perceived as both down-to-earth and ruthless, through he is also known as a devoted family man.

Business Lessons:

Ergen focuses everyone on his core business at all times, especially when deals are made and broken. In the satellite business, Ergen's goal is simple: to remain the best value at the best price.

- Make sure that people understand your vision and their part in it. Present it in appropriate terms to everyone involved.

• Keep your focus simple so that people can explain it quickly and accurately to colleagues and customers.

Key Strength:

Identifying and exploiting market potential to the full.

Best Decision:

Handing out free satellite dishes to woo customers away from a rival company.

Chung Mong-koo

Chairman, Hyundai-Kia

Hyundai was in trouble, when Chung took over as chairman of the automotive business. Its products were cheap, but consumers, the media and industry analysts knew why: Hyundai vehicles had a deserved reputation for poor quality. Within five years, Chung's obsession with improving the manufacturing process led to the start of a turnaround that has transformed Hyundai into one of the world's leading car makers. More recently, Chung has even bounced back from a conviction for embezzlement.

Biography:

Born in Seoul, South Korea, in 1938, Chung is the son of Hyundai's founder Chung Ju-yung. He graduated from Hanyang University, Seoul.

Low Expectations:

Few commentators expected much from Chung when his father, Hyundai's founder Chung Ju-yung, named him his successor as head of the automotive arm of the immense family-run conglomerate. He had drawn little attention in his 24 years running Hyundai's after-sales service unit, and he was not expected to deliver the turnaround the company badly needed.

From Joke to Powerhouse:

Even company insiders admit that, when Chung took over, the Hyundai brand was worthless. It had become connected with poor quality, Hyundai vehicles ranked among the worst in the world in terms of initial defects and they were unlikely to be seen anywhere outside South Korea.

Chung announced his intention to employ the same intense focus on quality that Toyota had used decades before to overcome the cheap-import stigma. Styling was upgraded and the company's research and development budget was doubled, but the highest priority of all was given to faultless manufacturing. Chung transformed Hyundai, turning the company and its affiliate, Kia Motors, into major global competitors. Within five years, Hyundai had become the world's fastest-growing car maker and was ranked second in a leading survey of quality.

Its stylish, well-priced and reliable vehicles were closing in on the best-known brands in prime markets around the world, including China. In 2007, Chung was convicted of embezzlement, taking money from Hyundai to run slush funds. His initial sentence of three years in jail was reduced to community service and a $1-billion donation to charity. He was remained in the driving seat at Hyundai.

Leadership Style:

Hard-nosed, detail-oriented, with a taste for micro-management. Chung gathers information quickly and has the charisma and reputation to impose his will on the company.

Business Lessons:

Sometimes companies overlook the simplest things. Hyundai had expanded rapidly by turning out cars quickly and cheaply; quality had never before been considered an issue. By making it the only issue, Chung turned a target of derision into a serious global force.

- Make people proud of what they do by rewarding excellence and challenging mediocrity.

- Set out up to five “principles” for people to work within; put quality at the top of the list.
- Implement a quality improvement programme; get everyone analyzing problems and finding solutions.

Key Strength:

Recognizing that quality could be as strong a driver of growth as quantity or price.

Best Decision:

To heighten attention to detail in Hyundai’s manufacturing and improve its products poor reputation.

Craig A. Dubow

Chairman, President and CEO, Gannett

Taking the helm of one of the biggest newspaper groups in the US, at a time of major crisis in the industry, Dubow's innovations have led the way in the industry's efforts to deal with a rapidly changing marketplace.

Biography:

Born in 1954. Dubow graduated from the University of Texas in Austin.

When Dubow, a Gennett veteran of eleven years, took over in 2005, newspapers had already been written off in many quarters as a dying dinosaur of an industry, a lumbering twentieth-century phenomenon destined for destruction at the heads of the the fast-moving, user-driven world of the Internet. Newspaper circulations have continued to decline since then, but Dubow has taken on the challenge of transforming a company built for different times into one fit for a world of new media.

His key initiative has been to reinvent newsrooms as "information centers", aimed at distributing news and comment through a variety of media, whether newspapers, broadcasting or online, offering a flexible, responsive service that can combine the power of a large newspaper company with the immediacy of the internet. Gannett and the newspaper industry still have a long way to go to take on new media and re-assert old formats, but Dubow has at least begun a fight back.

Best Decision:

Launching a comprehensive strategy to reinvent the old newspaper newsrooms as a system of "information centres".

Business Lessons:

Combine the new with the strengths of the old - Dubow's attempt to link new media with his company's traditional strengths indicate that all is not yet lost for newspapers.

David Packard

Co-founder,
Chairman and CEO
(1964-68), HP

One of the pioneers of technology, Packard was the co-founder of Hewlett-Packard (HP), an electronics and computer company that started out from a garage in Palo Alto, California, in 1939, and grew into a multibillion-dollar enterprise. With his partner William Hewlett, Packard created a business style and formula for success that became the prototype for Silicon Valley. He entered politics for a short time, serving as US deputy secretary of defense from 1969 until 1971, when he resumed his career at HP as chairman of the board.

Biography:

Born in 1912, in Pueblo, Colorado, Packard showed an early interest in electronics, becoming treasurer of the local radio club at the age of 12. At Stanford University, California, he graduated in 1934 with a bachelor's, followed by a master's degree in electrical engineering in 1939. Died in 1996.

Small Beginnings:

As an undergraduate at Stanford, Packard met fellow student William Hewlett and they made a pact to go into business together. In 1938, with just $538 in capital, he and Hewlett started a business in Packard's garage to market a resistance capacity audio oscillator (a sound equipment tester) that Hewlett had created as a graduate student. Working into the night, they finally developed the product, the HP200A, which they sold to Walt Disney Studios. Disney used the equipment to fine tune the soundtrack of the animated movie Fantasia.

Going International:

The two partners drew on their individual strengths to grow the company, and HP expanded beyond the garage in 1947. Packard was a great administrator and, together with Hewlett, he put into place the management practices that would later earn them recognition as pioneers of Silicon Valley. Their open-door policy and "management by wandering around" was known as "The HP Way" and helped set the standard for modern business management.

In 1957, Packard took the company public and established a manufacturing plant in Germany and European headquarters in Switzerland. Packard left in 1969 to serve in the Nixon government; on his return he found HP on the verge of borrowing $100 million to cover a cash-flow crisis. Within six months, Packard turned things around and the company was back in the black. He was less involved in the 1980s, when HP moved into computers and printers, but when earnings dipped nearly 11 per cent in 1990, he stepped in to oversee a major restructuring and boost to profits.

Leadership Style:

High-tech visionary, candid, no-holds barred. Packard was the architect of an open-door management style that was aimed at encouraging employee innovation.

Business Lessons:

Trusting in his own, his partner's, and his employee's new ideas, Packard allowed them the freedom to create and innovate. This was at the forefront of a move away from traditional business practices.

- Join the new wave of business thinking by trusting your people.

- Manage by "wandering around". If you are not getting out and listening to your staff, you are ignoring the people who will take you forward.
- Make sure your people never compromise on quality. Get them to act as if their name was on the label.

Key Strength:

Trusting the ability of others and nurturing their creativity.

Best Decision:

Going public with the company and expanding the manufacturing operation to Europe.

Estee Lauder

Founder and CEO,
Estee Lauder

Anything but a typical CEO, Lauder entered the realm of legend long before her death in 2004. In contrast to her working class upbringing in a shabby district of the New York borough of Queens, her cosmetics creations evoked elegance, luxury and ultra-femininity. By carefully tending the image, Lauder made consumers what to be like her and convinced millions that buying her products was the key. In 1998, she was the only woman on Time Magazine's list of the 20 most influential business geniuses of the 20th century.

Biography:

Born in 1906 in New York, Josephine Esther Mentzer was the youngest of six children of European immigrants, who lived above their hardware store in Queens. She claimed her family always called her Esty, but when a public school official spelled it Estee, the name stuck. Died in 2004.

Humble Beginnings:

Lauder began by selling skin-care products made by her Hungarian uncle, John Schotz, during the 1930s. She went on to mix, package and sell them herself at beauty salons, resorts and department stores. She was even known to stop women on the street to sell to them. Her breakthrough came in 1948 when she talked Saks Fifth Avenue into giving her counter space for her products. Her husband Joseph Lauter (the family changed their name to Lauder in the late 1930s) and their elder son worked with her in a rented office to meet the sudden increase in demand for her products.

No-One Outsold Her:

When Lauder set up her first office, in 1944, she added lipstick, eye shadow and face powder to her line of skin creams. She criss-crossed the United States in the 1950s, marketing her products to high-end department stores and later training their saleswomen. She created her first fragrance and bath oil in 1953.

Throughout the 1950s and 1960s, she continued to add products and develop new lines. She also launched the concept of "the Lauder look", the iconic face of the moment. By 1988, it was doing business in more than 100 countries and the Lauder family's shares were worth $6 billion.

While she exuded an aura of casual luxury, Lauder was a shrewd businesswoman. When the company was floated in 1995, it was done in such a way as to avoid a $95 million tax bill for her family – leading to a revision of the federal tax law two years later. She remained CEO until 1983 and chairman until 1995.

Leadership Style:

Ambitious, lavish, attentive to detail. The ultimate entrepreneur, Lauder did it all himself.

Business Lessons:

Obsessed with quality, and a shameless self-promoter, Lauder once explained her philosophy this way: "I have never worked a day in my life without selling. If I believe in something, I sell it and I sell it hard."

- Demonstrate the business and personal benefits of your products to customers to make your people passionate about what they do.
- Inculcate the "We are all salespeople" culture into your whole organization.

• Every activity starts when someone has sold something to a customer – there is no business without sales.

Key Strength:

She combined work and family while growing what she described as a "nice little business."

Best Decision:

Lacking sufficient advertising budget, she promoted her products by giving away free gifts to customers.

Francisco Gonzalez Rodriguez

CEO, BBVA

Former Computer programmer and stockbroker Gonzalez is now a leading figure in Spanish banking. Between 1996 to 1999, he was head of the Argentaria Group, where he led the successful privatization of the formerly government-owned group. As CEO of the newly merged Banco Bilbao Vizcaya Argentaria (BBVA), Gonzalez stabilized the troubled company, brought in transparency and ethical standards, embraced new technology, and expanded into Latin America. BBVA is now one of the largest banking groups in Spain.

Biography:

Born in Chantada, Spain, in 1944. Gonzalez obtained a degree in economics from Madrid's Complutense University.

From Computing to Banking:

Gonzalez first worked in computing, but left for a career in stock broking. He started his own company, FG Inversiones Bursatiles, in the late 1980s, building it into one of Spain's largest independent brokerages. In 1996, he sold it to Merrill Lynch for $30 million and moved into banking, as chairman of Argentaria, a company in its final privatization phase, and it was Gonzalez's job to get it into shape before the sale took place. He restructured management, cut jobs, refinanced assets, and the group was privatized in 1999.

Restoring Confidence:

After the 1999 merger of Argentaria with Banco Bilbao Vizcaya, Gonzalez became co-CEO of BBVA. Within a year, he faced one of the biggest crises of his career, when details of BBV's illicit activities, including money laundering, slush funds and bribery came to light. Gonzalez was not implicated, but he was left to deal with one of Europe's biggest scandals, which he did swiftly, closing secret accounts, paying taxes on the funds, and reporting all financial dealings to the Bank of Spain. Co-CEO Emilio Ybarra was among many executives forced to resign, and Gonzalez was left in charge.

To restore public confidence, Gonzalez overhauled the group's governance, appointing newcomers to the board based on expertise rather than personal friendships. He led BBVA's expansion in Latin America, and the franchise today has operations in 15 countries. In 2004, Gonzalez took the bank into the US with the aim of wooing the Hispanic market, a shrewd diversification which has helped shield it through the financial crisis, by curbing exposure to the sub-prime debacle, and allowing the company to grow in relative safety.

Leadership Style:

Austere, technologically savvy and a workaholic, Gonzalez believes in delegating.

Business Lessons:

Gonzalez built on his experience in the computer industry to introduce new services in banking based on the latest technology. He saw the internet, electronic payment systems and mobile phones as a means to cut cost and free up time, improving the efficiency of the bank.

- Use new technology to increase efficiency and to enhance knowledge of your customers.
- Don't be put off by new technology – what's daunting now will, in a very short time, be commonplace.

• Innovative technology is not optional. Your business rivals will be adopting it, so don't get left behind.

Key Strength:

Integrity. Without it, Gonzalez would have been hard pressed to withstand the BBVA's banking scandal in 2000.

Best Decision:

Expanding into Latin America, giving BBVA a total of more than 28 million customers and a foothold in the lucrative US Hispanic market.

George W. Merck

President and Chairman, Merck and Co., Inc.

Under the leadership of its founder's son, Merck & Co. embarked on a programme of pioneering drugs research that helped create the model for the modern pharmaceutical company. George W. Merck's early recognition of the crucial importance of research and keeping the company focused on solving medical problems turned Merck & Co., founded in Germany but set up as an independent business in America after World War I, into an industry leader that has discovered and developed countless medical breakthroughs along the way.

Biography:

Born in 1894, in New Jersey, Merck was the son of George Merck Sr, who has come to America in 1891 to set up a local branch of the German drug company. Merck studied chemistry at Harvard. Died in 1957.

Just another Drugs Company:

Merck was obliged by the outbreak of World War I to abandon his plan to study for a doctorate in chemistry. Instead, he began working in the family company in New Jersey. Propelled to the role of president by his father's ill health ten years later, he found himself running a modest company turning out conventional drugs and chemicals in an industry that was regarded by scientific researchers as slightly distasteful.

technology. By the turn of the millennium, Cisco was the most valuable company in the world, with a market capitalization of $550 billion, but when the tech bubble burst, Cisco's value evaporated, dropping to $100 billion. Remarkably, Chambers survived, a testament not only to shareholders faith in him but also to the way in which he handled the calamity – he openly admitted his mistakes and was therefore allowed to carry on.

Future Growth:

Chairman since 2006, Chambers has continued to grow Cisco by acquiring companies such as Linksys and Scientific Atlanta. Diversifying into new markets such as Voice over Internet Protocol (VoIP), Ethernet switching, social networking and telepresence, he has successfully kept the company in pole position as the internet evolves. When demand and growth slowed as a result of the global credit crisis, Chambers announced his intention to continue to invest in emerging technologies and markets, even suggesting that an economic downturn might be a good time for further acquisitions.

Leadership Style:

Collegiate. In an industry famous for mavericks who lead by sheer force of vision or personality, Chambers is that great rarity, a relatively hands-off manager. He sets the strategy but lets his people achieve it.

Business Lessons:

Chambers was a successful junior basketball captain, despite not being a gifted player. According to his father, he realized that the only way for him to win was to attract more talented people to play on his team.

- Hire the best people: they are ambitious and sometimes more difficult to manage but they get results.
- Channel ambition using aggressive promotion that stretches people and makes them grow into their jobs.
- Understand that one of the key responsibilities of the CEO is to unleash the talent of people by listening to them and searching for new insights.

Key Strength:

Hanging on to top creative talent, often difficult people to manage.

Best Decision:

Sharing investor's pain after the dotcom crash of 2000. Chambers decision to take a nominal $1 salary while he set about rebuilding the firm not only kept him his job, it also kept shareholders on board.

Jorgen Vig Knudstorp

CEO, LEGO

Faced with running a cherished national institution, Knudstorp didn't hesitate to make the sweeping changes in staffing, production methods and product lines necessary to bring the LEGO brand into the 21st century.

Biography:

Born in 1968 in Denmark, a short distance from Billund, the home of LEGO, Knudstorp holds a PhD from Aarhus University.

Since its inception in the 1930s, the LEGO company has been synonymous with the founding Christiansen family. When former McKinsey consultant Knudstorp took over in 2004, he was only the second CEO from outside the family to run LEGO. Such a privilege might have caused a more prudent man to move slowly but Knudstorp recognized that LEGO needed swift, wholesale restructuring if the company was to survive.

LEGO had been hit hard by the move away from traditional children's games to the more hi-tech options offered by consoles and PCs. To offset vast financial losses ($300 million in 2004), Knudstorp implemented drastic job cuts and turned to cheaper factories in Eastern Europe to manufacture the pieces.

Within a year of his arrival, LEGO was back in the black. Under Knudstorp, the company has expanded into advanced robotic technology, move tie-ins such as the Star Wars range, and computer games in order to enhance LEGO's future profitability.

Best Decision:

Selling 70 per cent of the Legoland theme parks to the Blackstone Group in 2005, which dramatically cut costs.

Business Lessons:

Don't be afraid of change – Knudstorp recognized that LEGO had to move with the times. The focus on "nurturing the child" rather than pursuing profit could no longer remain in the cut-throat 21st-century toy market.

Junior John Ngulube

CEO, Munich Re of Africa

Former agriculturist Ngulube is the first black CEO of insurance firm Munich Re of Africa, and he pursued a double strategy of improving financial performance, and boosting the economic integration of the black community.

Biography:

Born in Zimbabwe, in 1957. Ngulube studied agriculture at the University of Zimbabwe, Harare.

Before settling in the insurance industry, Ngulube grew up wanting to be a tobacco farmer and spent five years working with the Zimbabwean Ministry of Agriculture. The responsibilities of family life encouraged him to go into business, and he joined Munich Re as an agronomist in 1987. The firm's then head was Ernest Kahle, a liberal businessman who supported the ANC and was a champion of black economic power at a very troubled point in South Africa's political history.

Since taking over as CEO, Ngulube has been successful in both his stated aims, with results for 2007 showing a 25 per cent rise in premium income to 3.2 billion, despite the global slowdown. Munich Re has consistently exceeded government-set targets for affirmative action, with some 50 per cent of its middle management comprising black people, 20 per cent of them female. Ngulube's firmly believes that developing the skills base of the black South African community is not only good for the company, but for the country too.

Best Decision:

Committing equally to financial performance and affirmative action, demonstrating that integration of the black community has fiscal as well as socio-political benefits.

Business Lessons:

Be progressive and help others – Ngulube is noted for his progressive views and belief in maintaining a great empathy with his staff and peers.

Klaus Kleinfeld

Former CEO
Siemens AG

Credited with turning Siemens into "a proper company", Kleinfeld took over as CEO in 2005. Kleinfeld disposed of under-performing subsidiaries and told workers to accept longer hours for less pay or lose their jobs. His reforms were opposed by the trade unions and some directors, but the impact was dramatic: sales rose by 16 per cent and profits leapt 35 per cent to just under $4 billion, while shares soared to a 40 per cent increase in just over two years. Leaving Siemens in 2007, he now heads up aluminium giant Alcoa.

Biography:

Born in Bremen, Germany, 1957. Kleinfeld received a PhD in strategic management from the University of Wurzburg.

Building a One-Stop Shop:

Kleinfeld began his career as a management consultant before joining Siemens in 1987, but it was his posting to the US in 2001 as COO that gave him his opportunity to shine. He noticed that the different fiefdoms within the Seimens empire did not work well together and customers were faced with conflicting advice and separate bills from different Siemens divisions. Kleinfeld brought them together on a project-wide basis to make sure customers worked with a single Siemens interface.

A Can-Do Boss:

In the US, Kleinfeld encountered a new corporate culture, and liked the "can-do" approach that favoured customers and shareholders. He took these ideas back to Germany with him when he was made CEO in 2005. The ideas were popular with shareholders, who saw profits and share value rise, but they were resisted by the unions and traditionalists in Germany's corporate power elite. When he sold off the company's under-performing mobile telephone handset subsidiary to a Taiwanese firm, Kleinfeld faced widespread criticism.

He later announced a tie-up with Nokia to create the world's second largest business telecommunications equipment manufacturer. The deal revealed a key aspect of Kleinfeld's approach: if you are not the market leader or its closest rival, it is not worth your company being in that business; scale is everything. Unfortunately, allegations of corruption allegations, not related to him, caused a delay in his contract being renewed and he resigned in protest in 2007. In May 2008, he was appointed CEO of the US aluminium company, Alcoa.

Leadership Style:

Tough, independent and resilient. Kleinfeld took on corporate Germany's consensus-minded establishment to boost profits at Siemens, but he left when his contract was not renewed due to allegations, unrelated to him, of corruption amongst Siemen's top management.

Business Lessons:

Kleinfeld dragged Germany into globalization asking, "Who is the company for, and how can it compete?"

His answer was that to survive, western workers must be as productive as those in the developing world.

- Avoid a situation where successful divisions subsidize failure in others – that is not a long-term strategy.

- Understand that in the new globalized world, there's nowhere to hide poor performance. The competition will find your weaknesses.
- Be bold and implement lower terms and conditions for people in areas where the competition is global.

Key Strength:

He has a flair for leadership itself, other saying what needs to be said, and doing what is necessary to improve the company rather than being diplomatic.

Best Decision:

The launch of Siemens One during his time as the company's chief in United States. It turned Siemens vast range of services and subsidiaries into a one-stop shop where customers could share the company's economies of scale. It was later rolled out in 40 countries.

Larry Ellison

Co-founder and CEO, Oracle

A combination of a keen insight into where the IT industry was heading, and a preparedness to attack competitors without mercy, enabled Ellison to turn Oracle, the company he founded, into one of the world's leading producers of computer programs for business applications, known as "enterprise software". His eye for the next big move, his ability to weather the tough times, and his relentless commercial aggression have made Oracle one of the gaints of the software industry, and ensured his place as one of its most prominent figures.

Biography:

Born in Manhattan in 1944, Ellison never knew his father and his unmarried mother, Florence Spellman, left him to be raised by an aunt and an uncle, Lillian and Louis Ellison, who had emigrated from the USSR. Louis Ellison had taken his name from Ellis Island.

Going West:

Ellison began studying physics at the University of Chicago in the 1960s but, seeing more enticing opportunities elsewhere, dropped out and moved to California to work in the emerging computer industry. In the 1970s, he started work on a database project for the CIA, the title of which, "Oracle", became the name for the company he co-founded in 1977 with Robert Miner and Edward Oates.

Serving a New Market:

Ellison's forward-looking development strategy enabled Oracle to grow strongly throughout the 1980s. As the market for business software expanded rapidly, Oracle released a string of highly successful products targeting this new market. By the late 1980s, Oracle was a public company and a seemingly ever-growing name in the blooming IT industry.

In 1990, however, the company was faced with a sudden financial loss due to an overstatement of earnings. Ellison demonstrated that he could deal with difficult conditions as well as good, laying off 10 per cent of the company's workforce and bringing in key new staff to bolster performance. From then on, showing an ever-aggressive approach to key competitors, he pursued a programme of organic growth.

Embarking on an ambitious acquisition campaign in 2006, Oracle spent a total of $19 billion in two years in the purchase of 21 firms to move the company into entirely new areas, including retail and business intelligence software, taking the fight directly to its competitors with the aim of squeezing them out of the new markets. These strategies sealed Oracle's position as a software giant and confirmed Ellison as one of the leading figures in an industry with no shortage of big names.

Leadership Style:

Combative and aggressive. Ellison keeps a tight grip on every aspect of the company and makes it abundantly clear that he runs Oracle.

Business Lessons:

Hit the opposition hard, and then hit them again – Oracle's success has been largely down to Ellison's taste for going after the competition wherever he can.

- Create a system for measuring yourself against the competition, and consider your strengths and weaknesses, as well as those of your competition, from the customer's perspective.

- Choose your competitive battleground and focus on winning key orders, even if profitability is questionable.
- Don't be afraid to consider removing a competing product from the marketplace by buying the company.

Key Strength:

An appreciation of the opportunity that the new world of business software offered, combined with the technical savvy to give this new market what it wanted.

Best Decision:

Moving into the business database software market early, gaining a crucial advantage over the competition.

Lakshmi Mittal

Chairman & CEO, ArcelorMittal

Lakshmi Narayan Mittal is an Indian born London based billionaire, well-known for his unsurpassable business feats, larger than life persona, and opulent indulgences. Always making headlines with his entrepreneurial achievements and opulent lifestyle, Lakshmi Mittal tops the list of Britain's richest men, and the sixth wealthiest person in the world today, as per the Forbes Magazine. An executive member of the board of directors for the World Steel Association, International Investment Council in South Africa, International Business Council, the International Iron and Steel Institute's Executive Committee and many other global forums, it comes as no surprise that he is one of the most influential and powerful figures in the world today. Lakshmi Mittal is the chairman and chief executive of ArcelorMittal, which is apparently the largest steelmaking corporation in the world. Apart from his steel grip over the global steel manufacturing business, and his many luxurious indulgences, Lakshmi Mittal is also applauded equally for his philanthropist ideas. He has raised and contributed funds to support various community projects in different nation.

Biography:

Born on 15 June 1950 at Sadulpur, in Churu district of Rajasthan, Lakshmi Niwas Mittal had a very humble upbringing. His grandfather worked for one of the leading industrial firms, whereas his father was a businessman. The family relocated to

Kolkata after his father joined a domestic steel company as a partner. Laxmi Mittal graduated in commerce from St. Xavier's College in Kolkata and joined the family business that also involved his two younger brothers Pramod Mittal and Vinod Mittal. A few years later, ambitious Mittal branched out of his family domestic business and moved to Indonesia only to emerge as world's biggest steel baron in the coming years.

Leadership Style:

His success largely rested on taking over unprofitable, state-owned mills and making huge turnovers by boosting the production. He has been solely responsible for the growth of the steel business at an international platform. Lakshmi was the first to introduce the concept of "mini-mills" and "direct reduced iron" (DRI) as an alternate for steel making. This in turn proved to be a successful business strategy that was responsible for the growth of his firms. He started his international operations in Indonesia and Trinidad and Tobago before he expanded to 14 different countries acquiring several steel plants around the globe. In 2004, he managed to acquire more than 20 firms in Soviet Union including Kazakhstan, Romania and Ukraine. He soon started to make more acquisitions in America. His merger and later takeover with Arcelor, which is one of the biggest steel plants in the globe, earned him the status of a powerful international steel magnet. Over the years, Mittal has earned distinction as world's top steel tycoon and has received a number of awards.

Best Decision:

Mittal Steel became the world's largest steel maker when he took over the US's largest steel producer – the International Steel Group. He then consolidated all his steel holdings into Mittal Steel.

Leslie H. Wexner

Chairman and CEO, Limited Brands

Self made billionaire Wexner is continually seeking out future trends. Initially built on women's clothing, his Limited Brands Empire is now focused on personal health and beauty products, such as lingerie, skin care and cosmetics.

Biography:

Born in Dayton, Ohio, in 1937. Wexner graduated from Ohio State University with a degree in business administration.

"Les" Wexner launched The Limited clothing company with a loan of $5,000 and opened his first shop in 1963, selling fashion to suit women's lifestyles. He used the proceeds of a 1969 IPO (initial public offering) to finance a massive expansion into shopping malls, and gradually built up a large retail empire including Victoria's Secret, La Senza, Bath & Body Works and Henri Bendel. He was known as an entrepreneur rather than a manager; Wexner's tendency to flit from project to project put The Limited in financial crisis by 1993.

Acting on the advice of Harvard professor Leonard R. Schlesinger, Wexnerr centralized financial management and marketing, sold off poorly performing brands and closed down more than 100 shops, changing the name to Limited Brands in 2002 to reflect the change in direction. Profits from clothing sales continued to decline, so Wexner sold his Express and Limited Stores in 2007 in order to focus on his personal health and beauty brands, Victoria's Secret and Bath & Body Works.

Best Decision:

Building the Easton Town Centre complex in Columbus, Ohio, in 1999, a pioneering residental, entertainment and commercial open-air mall.

Business Lesson:

Never hesitate to reinvent – since opening his first shop more than forty years ago, Wexner has continuously acquired brands, refocused them and targeted new audiences.

Jean-Paul Agon

CEO, L'Oreal

As the head of the world's largest cosmetics company, with revenues of over $20 billion, Agon oversees brands such as L'Oreal paris, L'Oreal Professional, Garnier, Lancome and Maybelline. Agon is a firm believer in the power of marketing – ads like L'Oreal's "Because I'm Worth It", featuring Penelope Curz, are known the world over. He believes beauty is "science in a jar" and has adopted a "global or nothing" strategy for all brands, while moving L'Oreal closer to a green and ethical stance.

Biography:

Born in 1956 in Paris. "He graduated from the Hautes Etudes Commerciales Business School in Paris and then joined L'Oreal as a sales representative.

The Makeover:

Agon started out as a sales rep for L'Oreal in the south of France, driving samples around in a Fiat 127. He got his big break in management oversea, overhauling the company's loss-making subsidiary in Greece, only to find that the company was in such bad shape that five people had refused the job before him. However, Agon was able to use the experience to learn about the business, and subsequently turn the subsidiary around. He cites the event as determinant to his career.

Because He's Worth It:

Under Agon, a newer, more open L'Oreal has emerged, championing more natural products and promising an alternative to animal testing. His predecessor, Lindsay Owen-Jones, credits Agon with "a new sense of dynamism".

He earns a very competitive salary, but will certainly be worth it if he can continue to find new avenues for growth in what many regard as a saturated market. Competition is fierce, with Procter & Gamble moving aggressively onto L'Oreal patch, but Agon says he is optimistic, given the rapid development of the emerging economies and the ageing world population.

He plans to continue the decentralized culture, with each division (comprising consumer, luxury, professional and active) running its own brands, stocked through a careful strategy of buying local brands and expanding globally. He acquired the Body Soap group in 2006.

The company's research arm is second to none. It is widely believed that if anyone in the industry is going to find ways to end animal testing, it will be L'Oreal under Agon.

Leadership Style:

A people person, charming and charismatic, Agon is a persuasive talker. "It's not just his charm," said Anita Roddick, who sold her Body Soap company to L'Oreal in 2006. "It's that he hasn't got that autocratic, hierarchical attitude that some have. He likes dialogue."

Business Lessons:

Agon believes that marketing beauty is an art that goes beyond the rational. He wants marketing at L'Oreal to be a "unique combination of intelligence and emotion, rigour and sensitivity, dreams and reality."

- Appeal to your customer's needs and they may buy your products; appeal to their 'wants' as well and they'll buy in larger quantities.

- Even in business-to-business transactions look for the personal benefits to the buyer.
- Make sure your marketing messages flatter people's intelligence; never talk down to them.

Key Strength:

Prepared to take radical decisions and explain why.

Best Decision:

His 2006 acquisition of Body Shop was a major coup. He persuaded Anita Roddick to get on board and help him make L'Oreal products more "natural".

Jeff Bezos

Founder and CEO,
Amazon.com

The founder of Amazon.com had childhood dreams of becoming a cowboy or astronaut. Instead, he unleashed an internet trading phenomenon on the world. In 1994, Bezos read that the internet was growing by 2,300 per cent a year and knew he had to find a way in. With money borrowed from friends and family, Bezos build an online retail empire in about five years and revolutionized the way the world shops. As well as books, music and DVDs, Amazon now sells a vast range of products, and is the world's biggest online retailer.

Biography:

Born in Albuquerque New Mexico, in 1964. He graduated from Princeton in 1986 with honors in electrical engineering and computer science.

Web Wunderkind:

Bezos knew there was a huge amount of money to be made on the internet but was initially unsure what type of business would work best. He researched the mail-order industry and decided on books, believing that the millions of titles in print offered enormous potential for sales. On 6th July 1995, Bezos launched Amazon.com, with financial support from family and friends. The company operated out of the garage at his home in suburban Seattle, Washington.

The Power of Passion:

The business was a runaway success from day one. "It was obvious that we ever dared to hope," says Bezos. By the end of 1999, Amazon.com was a multibillion-dollar corporation selling 3.5 million titles via its pioneering website.

Amazon had fundamentally changed shopping and was a role model for a new generation of e-commerce whiz-kids worldwide. Then came the dotcom share crash. Bezos says he went from "internet poster boy to internet pinata." In 2000, Amazon – still investing heavily in infrastructure – lost $1.4 billion. While other online businesses were bankrupted in the crash. Bezos held on by putting in place dramatic cost-cutting measures, including shedding 1,300 staff. By 2001, Amazon was able to post a net profit of $5.1 million.

Bezos is a rare CEO who can claim to have pioneered a completely new industry from scratch. No longer just a book store, Amazon has expanded to sell a diverse array of goods from scientific supplies to groceries, and Bezos is positioned to revolutionize books themselves with the Kindle, an "iPod" of reading.

Leadership Style:

Pioneering and visionary, with a trademark guffawing laugh. Bezos is a charismatic leader whose innate confidence, enthusiasm and energy inspire colleagues to do their best.

Business Lessons:

Customers want three things, according to Bezos: the best selection, the lowest prices and the cheapest delivery. At Amazon, all decisions flow from these basic principles.

- Start with your customers and work backwards – what do they want?

- Put that customer strategy into simple terms and tell everyone to justify decisions against those criteria.
- Align your internet strategy with your customers needs and wants. Make sure that it echoes and develops your other channels.

Key Strength:

Bezos has made a billion-dollar global career out of knowing what customers want before they know it themselves.

Best Decision:

Introducing on-the-page customer reviews of products, helping would-be buyers to make their choices.

Jeff M. Fettig

Chairman, President and CEO, Whirlpool Corp.

Whirlpool has earned a strong reputation for its emphasis on innovation under Fettig's leadership. In a market often dominated by price, he has created a distinctive platform for growth in a tough industry.

Biography:

Born in Tipton, Indiana, in 1957. Fettig earned a bachelor's in finance and an MBA from Indiana University.

A career man at Whirlpool, Fettig was part of the leadership group in 1999 when former chairman and CEO David Whitwam decided that focusing on innovation was the best way for the company to advance in its tight markets.

When Fettig was appointed chairman, president and CEO in 2004, he intensified this approach, urging all employees to think of themselves as innovators and increasing the number of new products in development. His intention was to attract consumers by offering products that stood out from the "white goods" crowd.

Within a year, the company had trebled the volume of sales from new products, while plans were on target to continue boosting their share of activity to become the main plank of Whirlpool's operations.

The success of this approach soon became apparent. Within three years of Fettig's arrival in the top job, the share price had risen by more than 50 per cent and Whirlpool had been recognized as one of the most innovative companies in the US.

Best Decision:

Deciding to make new products the main focus of operations.

Business Lessons:

Find a new differentiator – in white goods, cutting prices is the usual way to increase sales. However, Fettig showed that innovation can be just as effective.

Jeff Raikes

CEO, The Bill and Melinda Gates Foundation

The unsung hero of Microsoft, Raikes created Microsoft Office, and made Windows the main profit generator of the most influential company of the past 30 years. Today he leads the Gate's mission to promote global equity.

Biography:

Born in Nebraska in 1948. Raikes won a bachelor of science in Engineering-Economics Systems from Stanford University.

When Bill Gates, co-founder of Microsoft, decided the world needed an industry-standard operating system, Apple was the best on offer. It was Raikes who wrote to Apple suggesting the companies collaborate. This offer was regarded as a ploy and rejected, leaving Microsoft to develop its own operating system that could work on any non-Mac. While Gates's vision underpinned its success, it was Raikes who made the system work. He asked the difficult questions, and then created the software package, Microsoft Office, that would bring in the money.

It is because of Raikes that most executives use Powerpoint for their presentations, Excel for their spreadsheets and Word for their documents. In 2008, after record quarter revenues of $16 billion, largely driven by his Business Division, which still accounts for more than a third of Microsoft profits, Raikes left to become CEO of the Bill & Melinda Gates Foundation. Its asset trust endowment stands at more than $35 billion.

Best Decision:

Bundling together Microsoft's word processing, spreadsheet and presentation applications as MS Office, the source of much of the company's profits.

Business Lessons:

Give the customers what they want – In this case an "industry-standard" operating system (Microsoft Windows) and business software package (Microsoft Office).

Jiang Nanchun

Founder, Chairman and CEO
Focus Media

Described as charismatic and visionary by colleagues, Jiang is the founder and former CEO of Focus Media, the biggest digital signage company in China. He is one of China's richest IT entrepreneurs.

Biography:

Born in Shanghai, China, in 1973. Jiang graduated from Huadong Normal University with a bachelor's degree in Chinese language and literature.

In 2003, "Jason" Jiang joined Aiqi Advertising and transformed it into Focus Media, providing outdoor advertising on LCD displays. As chairman and CEO, Jiang designed the first LCD device himself and secured six-month trials on 50 buildings in Shanghai. He sold slots to major firms including Hennessy, FUJI FILM, TAG Heuer and China Netcom, and then secured $500,000 of funding from Softbank China Venture Capital, which in turn attracted a further $4.2 million in Venture Capital. This enabled Jiang to target buildings in Beijing, Shenzhen and Guangzhou as well as installing screens in supermarkets and airport shuttle buses.

By late 2005, the company had 35,000 LCD screens in 52 major cities. A successful initial public offering in 2005 enabled Jiang to acquire rivals Frame Media and Target Media. Excellent results in 2007 were followed by a disappointing year in 2008, and Jiang was replaced by Tan Zhi, who in late 2008 oversaw a $1 billion M&A deal with online media company Sina Corp.

Best Decision:

Acquiring Allyes Information Technology Company in 2007, allowing Focus Media to enter the world of internet advertising.

Business Lessons:

Learn to delegate – although Jiang built the business from scratch, he handed over the day-to-day running of Focus Media in the interest of good management.

Jochen Zeitz

CEO, Puma AG

The youngest person ever to head a company on the German Stock Exchange, Zeitz was just 29 in 1993 when he became CEO of Puma. Many in the industry gave him little chance of turning around the ailing shoemaker, which was sinking under the weight of an outdated product line and $100 million in debt. Zeitz's combination of hard-headed cost-cutting and a flair for freewheeling innovation not only made Puma one of the world's hottest fashion brands but also created an entirely new market for sport-style leisurewear.

Biography:

Born in Mannheim, Germany, in 1963. He graduated from the European Business School with a degree in international marketing and finance in 1986.

A Bold Bet:

After training as a marketer at Colgate-Palmolive, Zeitz joined Puma as business manager of footwear marketing in 1990. He rose rapidly as the company went through three CEOs in two years, and when the role came up once again, the company took a bold bet in hiring to youthful and dynamic Zeitz in the hope that he could provide the new ideas needed to put an end to eight straight years of losses.

Sport Meets Fashion:

Zeitz began by applying the classic cost-cutter's medicine. He laid off staff and closed unprofitable production lines and warehouses, and in 1994 produced Puma's first profit since 1986. He continued with the tough treatment for another three years, stripping away bureaucracy, cutting the workforce almost in half, and shifting production to Asia, creating a learner, more nimble company.

He then made the key move of repositioning the brand, acknowledging it would never outstrip giant rivals Adidas and Nike. This was a bold stroke that changed the company's emphasis from sports performance to fashion and lifestyle. Instead of trying to compete directly over the sporting usefulness of its products, Puma emphasized colour, line and style. He brought in a range of high-profile designers to create and promote new products, crafting a cool, rebellious yet retro image that made Puma a hot fashion property.

As a direct result of his strategy, the fashion sportswear side became the heart of the resurrected company, bringing high levels of profitability and altering the nature of the sportswear market, as competitors reoriented themselves towards leisurewear too.

Leadership Style:

Obsessive and controlling. Zeitz likes to take care of the details. He even operated as his own board-level finance director for much of his time as CEO.

Business Lessons:

Going head-to-head with stronger competition in your core products isn't always the best way forward. Maybe those core products can be redesigned and re-launched. You might even create a new market.

- If you are continuously playing catch-up with a competitior, work out how to change the game.

- Look for brand "width". To which markets would your brand name give you instant access?
- Try building new markets by experimenting with your existing consumer base; you'll soon find out if you have created a new demand.

Key Strength:

Having the marketing vision to see how sportswear could be made cool.

Best Decision:

Hiring top designer Jill Sander to produce a line of fashion shoes in 1998.

John T. Chambers

Chairman and CEO,
Cisco Systems

A superb salesman who has put Cisco networking equipment at the heart of the internet, Chambers has turned the firm into an IT giant. So central is Cisco Systems technology to the internet, he can justifiably be considered one of the most significant figures in the evolution of the new medium. Chambers has demonstrated a rare understanding of the management of corporate acquisitions, acquiring network specialists StrataCom and Cerent among others, and enabling Cisco to weather the bursting of the dotcom bubble.

Biography:

Born in Cleveland, Ohio, in 1949. He holds a bachelor's degree in business studies and a law degree from West Virginia University, and an MBA from Indiana University.

Technology Leader:

Chambers became CEO of Cisco in 1995, after 20 years in IT sales for IBM and Wang Labs. A natural communicator, he soon made his name as an enthusiast who believed the net world change the way the world works, lives, plays and learns. He made sure that Cisco took a leading role in making that happen, buying up firms like StrataCom and Cerent in order to build a dominant footprint in the online infrastructure market.

Chambers also attracted top people to the company and proved himself a natural manager, as interested in people as technology. By the turn of the millennium, Cisco was the most valuable company in the world, with a market capitalization of $550 billion, but when the tech bubble burst, Cisco's value evaporated, dropping to $100 billion. Remarkably, Chambers survived, a testament not only to shareholders faith in him but also to the way in which he handled the calamity – he openly admitted his mistakes and was therefore allowed to carry on.

Future Growth:

Chairman since 2006, Chambers has continued to grow Cisco by acquiring companies such as Linksys and Scientific Atlanta. Diversifying into new markets such as Voice over Internet Protocol (VoIP), Ethernet switching, social networking and telepresence, he has successfully kept the company in pole position as the internet evolves. When demand and growth slowed as a result of the global credit crisis, Chambers announced his intention to continue to invest in emerging technologies and markets, even suggesting that an economic downturn might be a good time for further acquisitions.

Leadership Style:

Collegiate. In an industry famous for mavericks who lead by sheer force of vision or personality, Chambers is that great rarity, a relatively hands-off manager. He sets the strategy but lets his people achieve it.

Business Lessons:

Chambers was a successful junior basketball captain, despite not being a gifted player. According to his father, he realized that the only way for him to win was to attract more talented people to play on his team.

- Hire the best people: they are ambitious and sometimes more difficult to manage but they get results.
- Channel ambition using aggressive promotion that stretches people and makes them grow into their jobs.
- Understand that one of the key responsibilities of the CEO is to unleash the talent of people by listening to them and searching for new insights.

Key Strength:

Hanging on to top creative talent, often difficult people to manage.

Best Decision:

Sharing investor's pain after the dotcom crash of 2000. Chambers decision to take a nominal $1 salary while he set about rebuilding the firm not only kept him his job, it also kept shareholders on board.

Jorgen Vig Knudstorp

CEO, LEGO

Faced with running a cherished national institution, Knudstorp didn't hesitate to make the sweeping changes in staffing, production methods and product lines necessary to bring the LEGO brand into the 21st century.

Biography:

Born in 1968 in Denmark, a short distance from Billund, the home of LEGO, Knudstorp holds a PhD from Aarhus University.

Since its inception in the 1930s, the LEGO company has been synonymous with the founding Christiansen family. When former McKinsey consultant Knudstorp took over in 2004, he was only the second CEO from outside the family to run LEGO. Such a privilege might have caused a more prudent man to move slowly but Knudstorp recognized that LEGO needed swift, wholesale restructuring if the company was to survive.

LEGO had been hit hard by the move away from traditional children's games to the more hi-tech options offered by consoles and PCs. To offset vast financial losses ($300 million in 2004), Knudstorp implemented drastic job cuts and turned to cheaper factories in Eastern Europe to manufacture the pieces.

Within a year of his arrival, LEGO was back in the black. Under Knudstorp, the company has expanded into advanced robotic technology, move tie-ins such as the Star Wars range, and computer games in order to enhance LEGO's future profitability.

Best Decision:

Selling 70 per cent of the Legoland theme parks to the Blackstone Group in 2005, which dramatically cut costs.

Business Lessons:

Don't be afraid of change – Knudstorp recognized that LEGO had to move with the times. The focus on "nurturing the child" rather than pursuing profit could no longer remain in the cut-throat 21st-century toy market.

Junior John Ngulube

CEO, Munich Re of Africa

Former agriculturist Ngulube is the first black CEO of insurance firm Munich Re of Africa, and he pursued a double strategy of improving financial performance, and boosting the economic integration of the black community.

Biography:

Born in Zimbabwe, in 1957. Ngulube studied agriculture at the University of Zimbabwe, Harare.

Before settling in the insurance industry, Ngulube grew up wanting to be a tobacco farmer and spent five years working with the Zimbabwean Ministry of Agriculture. The responsibilities of family life encouraged him to go into business, and he joined Munich Re as an agronomist in 1987. The firm's then head was Ernest Kahle, a liberal businessman who supported the ANC and was a champion of black economic power at a very troubled point in South Africa's political history.

Since taking over as CEO, Ngulube has been successful in both his stated aims, with results for 2007 showing a 25 per cent rise in premium income to 3.2 billion, despite the global slowdown. Munich Re has consistently exceeded government-set targets for affirmative action, with some 50 per cent of its middle management comprising black people, 20 per cent of them female. Ngulube's firmly believes that developing the skills base of the black South African community is not only good for the company, but for the country too.

Best Decision:

Committing equally to financial performance and affirmative action, demonstrating that integration of the black community has fiscal as well as socio-political benefits.

Business Lessons:

Be progressive and help others – Ngulube is noted for his progressive views and belief in maintaining a great empathy with his staff and peers.

Klaus Kleinfeld

Former CEO
Siemens AG

Credited with turning Siemens into "a proper company", Kleinfeld took over as CEO in 2005. Kleinfeld disposed of under-performing subsidiaries and told workers to accept longer hours for less pay or lose their jobs. His reforms were opposed by the trade unions and some directors, but the impact was dramatic: sales rose by 16 per cent and profits leapt 35 per cent to just under $4 billion, while shares soared to a 40 per cent increase in just over two years. Leaving Siemens in 2007, he now heads up aluminium giant Alcoa.

Biography:

Born in Bremen, Germany, 1957. Kleinfeld received a PhD in strategic management from the University of Wurzburg.

Building a One-Stop Shop:

Kleinfeld began his career as a management consultant before joining Siemens in 1987, but it was his posting to the US in 2001 as COO that gave him his opportunity to shine. He noticed that the different fiefdoms within the Seimens empire did not work well together and customers were faced with conflicting advice and separate bills from different Siemens divisions. Kleinfeld brought them together on a project-wide basis to make sure customers worked with a single Siemens interface.

A Can-Do Boss:

In the US, Kleinfeld encountered a new corporate culture, and liked the "can-do" approach that favoured customers and shareholders. He took these ideas back to Germany with him when he was made CEO in 2005. The ideas were popular with shareholders, who saw profits and share value rise, but they were resisted by the unions and traditionalists in Germany's corporate power elite. When he sold off the company's under-performing mobile telephone handset subsidiary to a Taiwanese firm, Kleinfeld faced widespread criticism.

He later announced a tie-up with Nokia to create the world's second largest business telecommunications equipment manufacturer. The deal revealed a key aspect of Kleinfeld's approach: if you are not the market leader or its closest rival, it is not worth your company being in that business; scale is everything. Unfortunately, allegations of corruption allegations, not related to him, caused a delay in his contract being renewed and he resigned in protest in 2007. In May 2008, he was appointed CEO of the US aluminium company, Alcoa.

Leadership Style:

Tough, independent and resilient. Kleinfeld took on corporate Germany's consensus-minded establishment to boost profits at Siemens, but he left when his contract was not renewed due to allegations, unrelated to him, of corruption amongst Siemen's top management.

Business Lessons:

Kleinfeld dragged Germany into globalization asking, "Who is the company for, and how can it compete?"

His answer was that to survive, western workers must be as productive as those in the developing world.

- Avoid a situation where successful divisions subsidize failure in others – that is not a long-term strategy.

- Understand that in the new globalized world, there's nowhere to hide poor performance. The competition will find your weaknesses.
- Be bold and implement lower terms and conditions for people in areas where the competition is global.

Key Strength:

He has a flair for leadership itself, other saying what needs to be said, and doing what is necessary to improve the company rather than being diplomatic.

Best Decision:

The launch of Siemens One during his time as the company's chief in United States. It turned Siemens vast range of services and subsidiaries into a one-stop shop where customers could share the company's economies of scale. It was later rolled out in 40 countries.

Larry Ellison

Co-founder and

CEO, Oracle

A combination of a keen insight into where the IT industry was heading, and a preparedness to attack competitors without mercy, enabled Ellison to turn Oracle, the company he founded, into one of the world's leading producers of computer programs for business applications, known as "enterprise software". His eye for the next big move, his ability to weather the tough times, and his relentless commercial aggression have made Oracle one of the gaints of the software industry, and ensured his place as one of its most prominent figures.

Biography:

Born in Manhattan in 1944, Ellison never knew his father and his unmarried mother, Florence Spellman, left him to be raised by an aunt and an uncle, Lillian and Louis Ellison, who had emigrated from the USSR. Louis Ellison had taken his name from Ellis Island.

Going West:

Ellison began studying physics at the University of Chicago in the 1960s but, seeing more enticing opportunities elsewhere, dropped out and moved to California to work in the emerging computer industry. In the 1970s, he started work on a database project for the CIA, the title of which, "Oracle", became the name for the company he co-founded in 1977 with Robert Miner and Edward Oates.

Serving a New Market:

Ellison's forward-looking development strategy enabled Oracle to grow strongly throughout the 1980s. As the market for business software expanded rapidly, Oracle released a string of highly successful products targeting this new market. By the late 1980s, Oracle was a public company and a seemingly ever-growing name in the blooming IT industry.

In 1990, however, the company was faced with a sudden financial loss due to an overstatement of earnings. Ellison demonstrated that he could deal with difficult conditions as well as good, laying off 10 per cent of the company's workforce and bringing in key new staff to bolster performance. From then on, showing an ever-aggressive approach to key competitors, he pursued a programme of organic growth.

Embarking on an ambitious acquisition campaign in 2006, Oracle spent a total of $19 billion in two years in the purchase of 21 firms to move the company into entirely new areas, including retail and business intelligence software, taking the fight directly to its competitors with the aim of squeezing them out of the new markets. These strategies sealed Oracle's position as a software giant and confirmed Ellison as one of the leading figures in an industry with no shortage of big names.

Leadership Style:

Combative and aggressive. Ellison keeps a tight grip on every aspect of the company and makes it abundantly clear that he runs Oracle.

Business Lessons:

Hit the opposition hard, and then hit them again – Oracle's success has been largely down to Ellison's taste for going after the competition wherever he can.

- Create a system for measuring yourself against the competition, and consider your strengths and weaknesses, as well as those of your competition, from the customer's perspective.

- Choose your competitive battleground and focus on winning key orders, even if profitability is questionable.
- Don't be afraid to consider removing a competing product from the marketplace by buying the company.

Key Strength:

An appreciation of the opportunity that the new world of business software offered, combined with the technical savvy to give this new market what it wanted.

Best Decision:

Moving into the business database software market early, gaining a crucial advantage over the competition.

Lakshmi Mittal

Chairman & CEO,
ArcelorMittal

Lakshmi Narayan Mittal is an Indian born London based billionaire, well-known for his unsurpassable business feats, larger than life persona, and opulent indulgences. Always making headlines with his entrepreneurial achievements and opulent lifestyle, Lakshmi Mittal tops the list of Britain's richest men, and the sixth wealthiest person in the world today, as per the Forbes Magazine. An executive member of the board of directors for the World Steel Association, International Investment Council in South Africa, International Business Council, the International Iron and Steel Institute's Executive Committee and many other global forums, it comes as no surprise that he is one of the most influential and powerful figures in the world today. Lakshmi Mittal is the chairman and chief executive of ArcelorMittal, which is apparently the largest steelmaking corporation in the world. Apart from his steel grip over the global steel manufacturing business, and his many luxurious indulgences, Lakshmi Mittal is also applauded equally for his philanthropist ideas. He has raised and contributed funds to support various community projects in different nation.

Biography:

Born on 15 June 1950 at Sadulpur, in Churu district of Rajasthan, Lakshmi Niwas Mittal had a very humble upbringing. His grandfather worked for one of the leading industrial firms, whereas his father was a businessman. The family relocated to

Kolkata after his father joined a domestic steel company as a partner. Laxmi Mittal graduated in commerce from St. Xavier's College in Kolkata and joined the family business that also involved his two younger brothers Pramod Mittal and Vinod Mittal. A few years later, ambitious Mittal branched out of his family domestic business and moved to Indonesia only to emerge as world's biggest steel baron in the coming years.

Leadership Style:

His success largely rested on taking over unprofitable, state-owned mills and making huge turnovers by boosting the production. He has been solely responsible for the growth of the steel business at an international platform. Lakshmi was the first to introduce the concept of "mini-mills" and "direct reduced iron" (DRI) as an alternate for steel making. This in turn proved to be a successful business strategy that was responsible for the growth of his firms. He started his international operations in Indonesia and Trinidad and Tobago before he expanded to 14 different countries acquiring several steel plants around the globe. In 2004, he managed to acquire more than 20 firms in Soviet Union including Kazakhstan, Romania and Ukraine. He soon started to make more acquisitions in America. His merger and later takeover with Arcelor, which is one of the biggest steel plants in the globe, earned him the status of a powerful international steel magnet. Over the years, Mittal has earned distinction as world's top steel tycoon and has received a number of awards.

Best Decision:

Mittal Steel became the world's largest steel maker when he took over the US's largest steel producer – the International Steel Group. He then consolidated all his steel holdings into Mittal Steel.

Leslie H. Wexner

Chairman and CEO,
Limited Brands

Self made billionaire Wexner is continually seeking out future trends. Initially built on women's clothing, his Limited Brands Empire is now focused on personal health and beauty products, such as lingerie, skin care and cosmetics.

Biography:

Born in Dayton, Ohio, in 1937. Wexner graduated from Ohio State University with a degree in business administration.

"Les" Wexner launched The Limited clothing company with a loan of $5,000 and opened his first shop in 1963, selling fashion to suit women's lifestyles. He used the proceeds of a 1969 IPO (initial public offering) to finance a massive expansion into shopping malls, and gradually built up a large retail empire including Victoria's Secret, La Senza, Bath & Body Works and Henri Bendel. He was known as an entrepreneur rather than a manager; Wexner's tendency to flit from project to project put The Limited in financial crisis by 1993.

Acting on the advice of Harvard professor Leonard R. Schlesinger, Wexnerr centralized financial management and marketing, sold off poorly performing brands and closed down more than 100 shops, changing the name to Limited Brands in 2002 to reflect the change in direction. Profits from clothing sales continued to decline, so Wexner sold his Express and Limited Stores in 2007 in order to focus on his personal health and beauty brands, Victoria's Secret and Bath & Body Works.

Best Decision:

Building the Easton Town Centre complex in Columbus, Ohio, in 1999, a pioneering residental, entertainment and commercial open-air mall.

Business Lesson:

Never hesitate to reinvent – since opening his first shop more than forty years ago, Wexner has continuously acquired brands, refocused them and targeted new audiences.

Luiza Helena Trajano Rodrigues

CEO, Magazine Luiza

In the years that Rodrigues has been running Magazine Luiza, Brazil's third largest retail chain, she has revolutionized the retail landscape for poorer customers by introducing virtual showrooms and low-interest credit.

Biography:

Born in 1952 in Brazil. Rodrigues is the niece of the founders of the Magazine Luiza retail chain. She studied at the France Law School, Sao Paulo.

Aged 12, Rodrigues started a hoilday job at Magazina Luiza, the family-run store. In 1991, 27 years later, she was appointed CEO. Her first goal was to improve employee morale by giving power to store managers and sales teams, letting them set their own targets. She also granted low-interest credit and pioneered e-shopping in Brazil, opening "virtual showrooms" in rural areas and poorer urban neighborhoods.

Equipped only with high-speed computers on which to view the chain's products, they require just 15 per cent of the investment needed to set up a conventional store. With around 80 per cent of sales on credit, Rodrigues has faced criticism that her policies exploit the poor.

However, customers remain loyal and the default rate of clients is 50 per cent lower than the average for Brazil's retailers. Opening around 50 stores in the Sao Paulo metropolitan area,

Rodrigues had brought Magazine Luiza one step closer to displacing Ponto Frio as Brazil's second largest retailer.

Best Decision:

Reorganizing the management, replacing family members with a holding company and board to oversee day-to-day operations.

Business Lessons:

Innovation is the key – Rodrigues has consistently introduced new ideas, ensuring the company consistently turned to profit, despite Brazil's volatile economy.

Mark Zuckerberg

Founder and CEO, Facebook

The youngest-ever dollar billionaire, Zuckerberg has also made his fortune in record time. A Harvard dropout, he founded social networking site Facebook in February 2004, and a little over two years later he is reputed to have received an offer of $1 billion for the business from Yahoo! Lacking neither ambition nor self-confidence, the self-confessed programming geek turned the offer down. In 2007, Microsoft took a 1.6 per cent stake in Facebook, valuing the company at an incredible $15 billion.

Biography:

Born in White Plains, New York, in 1984. After attending New Hampshire's exclusive Phillips Exeter Academy, Zuckerberg went to Harvard to study Computer Science, but decided to drop out in 2004 to pursue Facebook full time.

College Whizzkid:

The website that would become Facebook was started by Zuckerberg as a place for his Harvard college mates to meet up online. Facebook was so successful that he dropped out to pursue the idea commercially. The quiet and thoughtful, if occasionally outspoken, Zuckerberg certainly knows how to impress.

His first backer was PayPal founder Peter Thiel, who has since been joined by Hong Kong billionaire Li Ka-shing. Growth has been explosive: with more than 150 million users it is now the number one social networking site and the fourth most visited website in the world.

Seeking Profitability:

A CEO in his early twenties, Zuckerberg lacks experience, but his vision and commitment, and his ability to attract likeminded colleagues to the company, have guided the business to runaway popularity. What started as a means of staying in touch with college friends has developed into a broader social network, a public and political forum, and even a search engine, as people tap their friends for advice and information. The Facebook site itself is continually being improved, and Zuckerberg even invites users to submit, and profit from, their own software, increasing what Facebook has to offer.

Zuckerberg insists that his key interest is in building the Facebook community rather than chasing money, a claim that his refusal to sell would seem to confirm. Facebook does not publish its financial performance figures, but it is widely thought to be cashflow negative. Zuckerberg's number one challenge for the future is to figure out a way to make money before his investors start to lose patience.

Leadership Style:

Perfectionist. Zuckerberg's desire to push the boundaries of what is possible online makes Facebook the employer of choice for a whole generation of top techies.

Business Lessons:

Facebook's meteoric rise is testament to Zuckerberg's vision, drive and ambition. His commitment to the website has been unwavering, its early success driving him forward. Zuckerberg is, in many ways, the public face of the company, and he has embraced the responsibilities that come with that role.

- Good ideas are ten a penny; everyone will have thought of them and the opportunities they raise.

• Single yourself out from the rest with your willingness to put in the hours and make things happen.

• Think a year ahead. Ask: "What innovation could I be kicking myself about when someone else does it?"

Key Strength:

Combining high-level technical skills with an understanding of the potential of the internet as a social rather than merely transactional medium.

Best Decision:

Going open source in 2007. This allowed anyone to create applications for Facebook users, providing a much enhanced service to Facebook users.

Mary Kay Ash

Founder and CEO
Mary Kay, Inc.

Inspiring and Empowering, Ash is widely regarded as the most successful female entrepreneur in US history. By basing her company around the needs and dreams of women employees, she created a new business model.

Biography:

Born in 1918 in Texas, Ash (nee Mary kathlyn Wagner) nursed her sick father as a teenager while her mother managed a restaurant. She studied at the University of Houston. Died in 2001.

When she was overlooked yet again for a top direct sales job in favour of a man she had trained, Ash quit the job. Over the years, she had developed her own theory of sales and marketing, and this became the business plan for Mary Kay Cosmetics, which she launched in 1963 using her $5,000 life savings. Forty-five years later, Mary Kay, Inc. had expanded to include 33,000 independent sales directors, and global wholesale sales topped $2.4 billion.

Ash achieved this by instigating a new corporate philosophy based on the bottom line, but on her "Golden Rule" of "praising women to success" and putting "God first, family second and career third". Her natural flair for public relations – she rewarded top saleswomen with pink Cadillacs – received national coverage. Ash recognized the importance of women's aspirations, and the company philosophy appealed to the sales force and customers alike. After her death in 2001, she was succeeded as CEO by her son Richard Rogers.

Business Lessons:

Accommodate family life and reward good work – Ash's positive approach to employment got the best out of her staff.

Best Decision:

Risking her life savings to set up her own business, and employing women with families to run it.

Ma Yun

Co-founder and CEO, Alibaba.com Ltd

Selected as one of the 25 most powerful business people in Asia by Fortune magazine in 2005, Ma, CEO and co-founder of Alibaba, the world's largest online B2B marketplace, is regarded as the pioneer of e-commerce in China.

Biography:

Born in Zhejiang Province, China, in 1946. Ma taught himself English and graduated from Hangzhou Teacher's institute in 1988.

It was when visiting Seattle as an interpreter with a trade delegation that "Jack" Ma was first exposed to the power of the internet. On his return to China, he began creating websites for friends. After a short spell as head of the China International Electronic Commerce Centre's Infoshare division, Ma raised $60,000 to set up a business-to-business website, Alibaba, in 1999. Its early years were difficult and Ma was forced to make layoffs when the dotcom bubble burst.

In 2003, however, an outbreak of SARS restricted travel in China but raised demand for online transactions, and Alibaba took off. That same year, Ma launched Taobao.com, a consumer-to-consumer auction website similar to ebay, which also incorporated an innovative online payment sevice, Alipay. In 2005, Ma acquired Yahoo! China, securing $1 billion of investment for Alibaba. Ma remains confident that Alibaba can survive times of economic crisis, and is committed to making Alibaba the world's largest e-commerce company.

Best Decision:

Taking Alibaba public in 2008, proving that a mainland Chinese company can be listed on the Hong Kong stock exchange and attract global investor interest.

Business Lessons:

Innovate or die – Ma has grown his company by addressing specifically Chinese market issues, rather than copying competitor's strategies.

Michael Dell

CEO, Dell, Inc.

The classic example of turning a personal obsession into an immense business success, Dell has become one of the leading figures in his generation's glittering pantheon of IT stars. From its beginnings in his university dorm room, his company broke the mould in the PC market, and Dell's innovative thinking and easy management style turned Dell, Inc. into a world market leader. When the founder stepped down as CEO, the negative effect on the company's fortunes was clear, and three years later he was back.

Biography:

Born in 1965 in Houston, Texas. His father was an orthodontist and his mother was a financial consultant and stockbroker. Dell dismantled an Apple computer and rebuilt it at the age of 15.

From The College Dorm:

While a student at the University of Texas in 1984, Dell began putting together PCs and selling them, a venture that proved so successful that, with a loan from his grandparents, he soon dropped out of college and set up the company that became one of the biggest players in the PC world. His innovative business grew so quickly that by the age of 27, Dell was the youngest CEO of a Fortune 500 company.

Going Direct:

Dell hit upon one simple idea that had not yet occurred to anyone else in the PC market – cut out the middle man. By selling PCs directly to customers, he was able to undercut the big guns of the industry, gaining market share rapidly and earning himself and his company a reputation as the customer's friend.

Dell's youthfulness and innovative streak made him a hot media favourite, while his emphasis on customer service increased Dell, Inc.'s popularity in the marketplace, and by 2002 the company was bringing in $35 billion in revenue. By 2004 it had become the world's largest PC maker, and the founder, feeling his job was done, made way for Kevin Rollins to become CEO, while remaining chairman. Dell had demonstrated that it is possible to build rapid success by creating a completely new business model. His refusal to confirm to the existing structures of his industry took outside-the-box thinking to an extreme and hugely successful conclusion.

In 2007, after the company had suffered a series of setbacks and had lost its number one spot in the market to Hewlett-Packard, Dell returned as CEO, determined to restore the fortunes of the company.

Leadership Style:

"Egoless". Dell has refused to take a reserved parking space or a door on his office. He applies the company's focus on customer service to the way it deals with its employees.

Business Lessons:

Dell showed that it is possible to be successful – and in a short span of time – working with a brand new business model. His non-conformist attitude has allowed the company to become truly innovative in its business models, with unprecedented results.

- Always accept that you could do things better than you are doing at the moment.

- Avoid accepting business practices whose only reason for existing is “we have always done it this way”.
- Keep shaking your organization up until you and your team are working in the best possible way.

Key Strength:

Going so far beyond conventional thinking as to establish a new business model.

Best Decision:

Selling his products direct to the consumer, leaving retailers out of the equation.

Muhammad Yunus

Founder and Managing Director, Grameen Bank

As founder of the micro-financing Bangladeshi Grameen Bank, Yunus is famed for giving the country's poor a hitherto unheard of leg-up into the world of entrepreneurship. Although the idea of micro-financing as an economic model to help the poor was not new, Yunus is lauded as the first to put the idea into action, first offering loans with government support in the late 1970s. In 2006, Grameen Bank and its founder were jointly awarded the Nobel Prize for Peace for their work in the eradication of world poverty.

Biography:

Born in Eastern Bengal (now Bangladesh) in 1940, Yunus was the third of nine children. He spent his early years in the village of Bathua but moved to the city of Chittagong in 1947, where his father had a successful jewellery business. He studied economics at Dhaka University and later completed a PhD in economics at the Vanderbilt University in Nashville, Tennessee.

A Spur to Charitable Action:

In 1972, Yunus left his position as assistant professor in economics at Middle Tennessee State University to return to Bangladesh. He joined the Department of Economics at the University of Chittagong, becoming professor in 1975. Influenced by his mother's charitable actions in his childhood,

Yunus took an active interest in the university's rural research programmes.

During a field trip in 1976, Yunus encountered villagers who were forced to borrow money from loan sharks at exorbitant rates to buy raw materials, which kept their earnings at subsistence level. Appalled, he took $27 from his own pocket and loaned in to 42 village women at low interest. The lower interest rates not only yielded markedly improved profit margins, but also encouraged personal initiative and enterprise.

From Idea to Reality:

Realizing that very small loans could make a real difference to those living on the edge, Yunus approached traditional banks, but despite offering to act as a personal guarantor, he was met with blank refusal. Undeterred, Yunus secured backing from the country's central bank and, after trial projects met with success, Grameen (meaning "rural" or "village" in Bangla) Bank came into existence as an independent bank in 1983.

Founded on the principles of trust and solidarity, the bank now has over seven million borrowers, primarily women, who also own 90 per cent of the bank's shares, the rest being owned by the Bangladesh government. The Grameen initiative has diversified into a range of ventures, including the Village Phone project, which has resulted in mobile phone ownership for some 260,000 people in rural areas.

Leadership Style:

Trusting and dedicated, Yunus possesses the capability to translate his visionary ideals into practical solutions.

Business Lessons:

Although Grameen loans are unsecured, repayment is 97 per cent – higher than any other banking system. Yunus encourages groups of borrowers to co-guarantee loans and support each other's enterprise efforts.

- Foster solidarity. Ensure contractors and sub-contractors are co-operating both financially and technically.

- Help individual borrowers, suppliers and customers to realize that a failure to act responsibly will have a knock-on effect on other businesses or individuals.
- Encourage your people to understand and protect the interests of their suppliers and customers.

Key Strength:

The determination to overcome the inertia of the traditional banking system.

Best Decision:

Making the initial micro-loans out of his own pocket.

Mukesh Ambani

CEO, Reliance Industries

No one personifies the shift of economic power from West to East better than Mukesh Ambani, one of the richest men in the world. His Reliance Industries, India's largest private sector company, has reached a market capitalization of more than $75 billion and ranks among the world's top companies. His steady management of business and political relationships has helped keep Reliance Industries centre stage as India opens up its communications, infrastructure and financial markets to the global economy.

Biography:

Born in Bombay (Mumbai) in 1957. Mukesh Ambani is the eldest son of the legendary tycoon Dhirubhai Ambani. A chemical engineering graduate from the University of Bombay, he also has an MBA from Stanford University.

Accepting the Challenge:

Ambani joined Reliance Industries, then a textiles company run by his father, Dhirubhai, in 1981. He helped his father to realize his dream of integrating his polyester fabric company backwards into petro-chemicals to control the supply of his own raw materials. Mukesh was given a huge challenge – to build one of the world's biggest oil refineries, in Gujarat. He lived on site and oversaw 85,000 staff in the construction of Jamnagar.

The project was delivered in two years at two-thirds of the cost of BP's smaller refinery in Malaysia.

Innovative Thinking:

In 2002, three years after Jamnagar was commissioned, Ambani repeated the trick when he launched Reliance Infocomm, this time demonstrating that he was a business innovator too. Reliance laid fibre optic cable, bought millions of super-cheap CDMA mobile phones from China, and sold 25 million handsets for $12 each to a market no-one had noticed – India's low earners, including street hawkers and ricksaw drivers. The death of Ambani Sr in 2002 led to bitter feuding between Mukesh and his younger brother Anil. The group divided in 2007 and Mukesh lost control of Reliance Infocomm.

Mukesh is particularly proud of his company's discovery of the Krishna-Godavari gas field in the Bay of Bengal, which is expected to produce 250,000 barrels a day, making a significant contribution to India's energy needs. Mukesh's current projects include a chain of supermarkets and two new cities on the outskirts of Mumbai and Delhi, providing much-needed infrastructure and creating up to five million jobs.

Leadership Style:

According to colleagues, his secret lies in delegation, but he also believes in rolling up his sleeves and getting his hands dirty. He retains huge amounts of detail, and at one point he was personally involved in the creation of 60 manufacturing facilities.

Business Lessons:

Learning a new industry takes time and effort. Ambani spent several nights a week sleeping on site in a steel truck container while he learned the oil business. He watched training videos during his morning workout.

- Observe footfall. In retail it pays dividends to note who goes past an outlet at different times of day.

- Spend as much time on competitor's websites as you do on your own. Even when you have an advantage people will catch up.
- Study your industry. Things change all the time, sometimes dramatically but more often by degrees.

Key Strength:

He is known in India as the ultimate project manager, able to realize business dreams in ambitious capital projects few would have the courage to try.

Best Decision:

Bringing mobile phone within the reach of even those earning a few dollars a day. In two and a half years he signed up ten million subscribers, quickly creating his own market.

Mukesh Jagtiani

CEO,
Landmark Group

Starting with a single baby goods store in Bahrain, Landmark Group founder and CEO Jagtiani has built up one of the largest retail chain in the Middle East, selling clothes, furniture, shoes and home ware. Now he controls more than 800 stores, which together comprise more than ten million square feet of retail area in countries across the Gulf, as well as Jordan, India, China, Spain, Pakistan and Egypt. Former college drop-out Jagtiani has come a long way from his humble beginnings and is now a multibillionaire.

Biography:

Born in Kuwait 1951, to Indian parents who had emigrated from Bombay (Mumbai). Jagtiani moved to London to study accountancy but dropped out of college.

Family Tragedy Strikes:

Sent to study accounting in London, "Micky" Jagtiani failed to stay the course. After a spell as a cab driver, Jagtiani swallowed his pride and returned to his family in Kuwait in 1972. Within a year, three close members of his family were dead – brother, father and mother. At 21 years, Jagtiani found himself with no family, no education and no job. Sorely tempted to go to India, his parent's home country, and devote his life to charity, Jagtiani instead decided to have a go at entrepreneurship.

Taking his $6000 inheritance, he flew to Bahrain and took over his late brother's shop. Recognizing that the Gulf had a large population of Asian expats who were traditionally overindulgent when it came to their kids, Jagtiani opened Baby Shop, selling toys and children's clothes and furniture. The business went from strength to strength as wave after wave of Asian and South Asian expats came to work in the region. Jagtiani opened more shops, and by 1992 had six stores and 400 employees.

The Move to Dubai:

In 1992, Jagtiani decided to move his family and company headquarters to Dubai. The timing couldn't have been better. Dubai was undergoing a massive building boom and transformation into a major business and tourist attraction. Despite being advised to turn his attention to the luxury market, Jagtiani stuck with his gut feeling and concentrated on middle-class consumers. Sales rocketed and Jagtiani diversified into home furnishing. More recently, he has branched out into restaurants and leisure. Landmark Group's annual turnover has topped $2.5 billion and continues to grow.

Leadership Style:

Affable, modest and charming. Jagtiani is a hands-on boss who expects his executives to spend time on the shop floor.

Business Lessons:

Jagtiani enforces the "category killer" concept, making sure that every brand his stores carry is the best in that sector. The stores themselves are based on the US and European models that many of his customers have experienced – spacious, with easy access and a large range of affordable products.

- Choose the best location in a geographic area with a large consumer market.
- Stock as wide a range of products as possible so that consumers have no need to shop elsewhere.
- Know your market: price products competitively to maintain customer loyalty.

Key Strength:

The intuition to spot a business opportunity. Jagtiani made the move to Dubai which enabled him to catch the Middle East's retail industry boom.

Best Decision:

Identifying the potential for baby products in the Middle East and focusing on that retail sector.

Naresh Goyal

Founder and Chairman, Jet Airways

The pioneer of India's private airlines, Goyal set up his own air travel agency, Jetair, in 1974. In 1993, he launched Jet Airways, hoping that India would soon liberalize its aviation industry. Today, Jet is India's largest airline.

Biography:

Born in Patiala, Punjab, India in 1949. Goyal moved to Delhi to work in his uncle's travel agency – a modest first step to building a hugely successful business.

As an international airline agent, Goyal understood the industry and as an Indian, he knew the frustration felt by India's middle classes towards the state-owned carriers. Persuading a group of Middle East investors to back him, he launched Jet Airways. It was a big gamble, but Goyal sensed that deregulation was in the air. Sure enough, India's state monopoly over scheduled air transport ended in 1994.

Jet has since put its rivals to shame with reliable flights and first-class cabin service, yet it operates on a break-even of 65 per cent seat sales – 20 per cent below that of many rivals. Goyal's ruthless cost control and commitment to high standards was reflected in the company's 200 IPO (initial public offering), which sold out in ten minutes, raising $260 million. This gave him the confidence to expand in a shrinking market when fuel costs soared. Goyal held his nerve and bought cheif rival

Sahara at a knock-down price. Jet has now moved to become a global operator.

Best Decision:

Pulling out of the deal to buy rival Air Sahara for $500 million in 2006, and clinching it for $340 million in 2007.

Business Lesson:

Sell your service – Goyal gambled on Indian air passengers being won over by a formula offering high-quality service, comfort, and reliability. He was proved right.

Nicholas W. Moore

MD, CEO, Macquarie Group Ltd

Financial vision and hard-nosed ambition are the hallmarks of Moore's approach to investment banking, which transformed the fortunes of Macquaire Bank, the Australian offshoot of UK investment house Hill Samuel, into a global investment banking and diversified financial services group. His innovations in restructuring business acquisitions helped bring 14 consecutive years of stellar returns to investors, although he has had to learn diplomacy the hard way, after a badly handled run-in with an Australian broadcaster in 2002.

Biography:

Born 1958. Moore attended the Catholic Saint Ignatius College in Riverview, Australia, before gaining a degree in commerce and law at the University of New South Wales.

The Art of the Deal:

Moore's greatest claim to fame was Macquarie's high-profile but unsuccessful bid for the London stock exchange in 2005. Dismissed as ill-considered and quixotic, the bid summed up Moore's expansionist tendencies and the love for deal-making that marked his tenure at the helm of the bank's Macquarie Capital arm. Moore embodied the go-getting financial culture of the 1990s and early 2000s, and the division thrived under his leadership, growing to deliver 60 per cent of the group's profits.

Macquarie became known as Australia's "Millionaires Factory" for the generous bonuses taken home by staff. Moore himself was most handsomely rewarded of all, becoming the country's second highest paid executive. Moore was the perfect foil for former CEO Allan Moss's cautious risk management approach.

Challenging Times:

Becoming CEO in 2008 after Moss retired, Moore continued to push for growth, acquiring US futures clearing outfit Shatkin Arbor in August of that year. But he took the helm just as times returned tough for leveraged players such as Macquarie, and soon faced the challenge of the global financial crisis. Macquarie announced record full-year profits of AU$1.8 billion in mid-2008, but profit fell significantly over the next six months.

Showing faith in the asset-trust business model, Moore set about rationalizing the business and reversing a precipitous fall in its share price by moving away from areas that offered lower returns, and cutting costs and staffing levels. Some observers regretted the departure of his urbane predecessor, but others saw Moore's tough approach and understanding of risk as ideal qualities for leading the bank in times of turmoil.

Leadership Style:

A risk-taker, Moore typifies the aggressive, entrepreneurial investment banker. Dubbed "cold and calculating", he is tough and focused, keeping his eye firmly on the deal.

Business Lessons:

Human capital is at the heart of Macquarie's success, as demonstrated by Moore's strategy of maintaining headcount and offering bonuses for good performance, even when the global economy stutters.

- Incentivize people but move away from big cash bonuses based on short-term performance, and instead offer longer-term, equity-based incentives.

- Your bonus scheme should emphasize an understanding of risk, so that staff are aware of the consequences.
- Bonus payouts attract media publicity. Make sure you can justify them by pointing to convincing results.

Key Strength:

Seeing the vast potential of under-exploited infrastructure and working out a way of exploiting it.

Best Decision:

Turning Macquarie's purchase of assets such as airports, toll roads, and care homes into listed trusts, the management of which has brought many years of record profit growth.

Paul Jacobs

CEO, Qualcomm, Inc.

With more than 25 patents under his belt, Jacobs is a leading innovator in the wireless technology field, and the man who has spearheaded Qualcomm's success in wireless telecommunications research and development.

Biography:

Born 1962. Jacobs gained bachelor's and master degrees in electrical engineering and a PhD from the University of California, Berkeley.

Having joined Qualcomm in 1990 as a development engineer leading the mobile phone digital-signal processor software team, Jacobs took over from his father as CEO in July 2005. Since then, he has been the primary driver behind Qualcomm's focus on wireless data services. Jacobs is a long-time advocate of 3 and 4G and social networking, and has driven the company's investment in new technology; its patents are an integral part of all 3G mobile networks.

Among his many successes are an improved relationship with telecommunications giant Nokia, the BREW effort (a popular software platform for mobile phones) and Qualcomm's development of mobile broadcast TV network MediaFLO, which provides live mobile television content via AT&T and Verizon Wireless, the two largest mobile operators in North America. Jacobs success has been proven by Qualcomm's results, with increase in both licensing and chipset divisions contributing to revenue of more than $11 billion.

Best Decision:

Resolving the firm's long-standing patent disputes with Nokia, resulting in a 15 year agreement, an upfront payment, and ongoing royalties, plus the ownership of a number of patents.

Business Lessons:

Keep on moving – Jacobs is consistently at the forefront of innovations, such as mobile broadcast TV network MediaFLO.

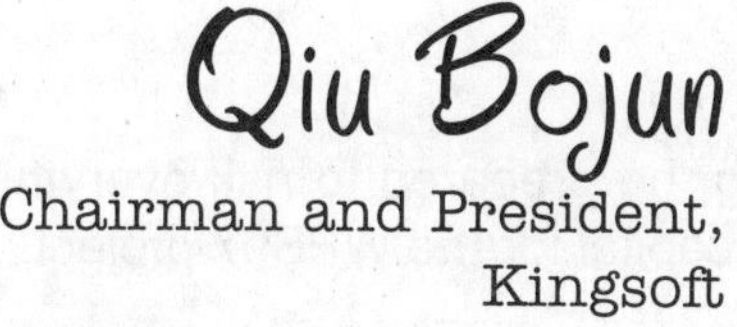

Chairman and President,
Kingsoft

Often referred to as the "Bill Gates of China", Qiu is president of the Chinese software company Kingsoft. A Han national, Qiu once turned down a job offer from Microsoft in order to develop the home software industry in China.

Biography:

Born in 1964 in China. Qiu graduated with a bachelor's degree in information systems from the National University of Defense Technology in Changsha.

In 1989, nine years after first using a computer, 25-year-old Qiu launched WPS, a Chinese-language word-processing programme. More user-friendly to Chinese script than imported software. WPS was an instant hit in China. In 1994, Qiu founded Kingsoft, but in 1996, lack of capital to fund the updated WPS97 project forced him to sell his family home. Fortunately, the software programme sold better than expected and in 1998, an injection of capital from the Lenovo Group resulted in a restructure, with Qiu Bojun becoming chairman and president.

Since then, Qiu has shifted the emphasis from software development to internet-based technology, with three major divisions: WPS, anti-virus programs and online games. Known for its innovative R&D, Kingsoft is a leading producer of online games in China, and has been trading on the Hong Kong stock exchange since 2007. Qiu is the company's biggest shareholder, with more than 20 per cent of the shares.

Best Decision:

Exploiting the niche for Chinese-language products. This led to great gains in a market that until then had been dominated by Roman-script software.

Business Lessons:

If you believe in something, be prepared to risk everything – Qiu sold his home to raise capital for the WPS97 project.

Ratan Tata

Chairman and CEO,
Tata Group

The company headed by Tata has almost single-handedly built Indian industry. Initially mill owners, the group now includes India's largest software house and one of its most prestigious hotel chains (the Taj), as well as steel and car production. The success of the Tata Group, India's largest conglomerate, is largely down to Tata's courageous and principled management strategies, and yet Ratan himself does not appear on any rich list; the Tata family owns just one per cent of the holding company.

Biography:

Born in Bombay (Mumbai), India, in 1937. Tata trained as an architect at Cornell University, New York State, and took a management course at Harvard.

A Slow Starter:

Early business failures in the Tata Group's electronics and mill interests did not mark Ratan out for a starring role. Indeed, when he succeeded his uncle, J.R.D. Tata, as chairman in 1991, few expected the group to survive the challenges of liberalization. By trimming the group's 300 "fiefdoms" and removing managers who didn't share his "global not local" vision, Tata reinvented the company.

Global Player:

Today, the Tata Group has the largest market capitalization of any business house of the Indian Stock Market. His ambitious global acquisition spree began in 2000 with the takeover of Tetley Tea. The 2007 purchase of Anglo-Dutch steel gaint Corus for $13 billion was the biggest takeover of a foreign company by an Indian corporate, marking his arrival as a truly global player.

It is often said that Tata's heart is in the motor industry. Famously media shy, Tata was propelled into the spotlight in 2008 with his bold takeover of prestige British brands Jaguar and Rover, a move that was branded as "reverse colonialism". In 1998 he launched the Indica, the first totally Indian car. With typically unwavering belief in his project to create a people's car, Tata proved skeptic wrong in 2008 with the launch of the "one lakh" ($2,150) car, the Tata Nano.

Under Tata's leadership, the group has set a standard for corporate responsibility. As well as providing housing, education and medical care to employees, the company ploughs over two thirds of profits into trusts that finance good causes. Unusually in India, the company is known to be incorruptible.

Leadership Style:

Audacious, degnified and philanthropic. One of Tata's first principles in business is to be bold but to "do no harm".

Business Lessons:

Tata believes passionately in using his company's growth for the betterment of his employee's lives and the community at large. He believes the company's long-term position and influence depend on this approach, and that shareholders will prosper in such a regime.

- Avoid all corrupt activities even when times are difficult and temptation is high.
- Obey your instincts when they tell you that what you are being offered is too good to be true.

- Make sure your company listens to the community around it and contributes to its well-being.

Key Strength:

The ability to think globally. Tata has transformed a lumbering, bureaucratic, Empire-rea conglomerate into a dynamic world player.

Best Decision:

Deciding that Tata Group should make its own cars. Critics said it was vanity project, but Tata Motors is now India's second biggest car maker.

Richard D. Fairbank

Founder, Chairman and CEO, Capital One

Focused and tenacious, Fairbank transformed the American credit card industry in the 1990s with innovative ideas such as "teaser rates" and zero-interest balance transfers drawing customers to Capital One.

Biography:

Born in California in 1950. Fairbank received an MBA from the Stanford Graduate School of Business.

Richard Fairbank started his career in 1981 as a management consultant with Strategic Planning Associates. He began developing the idea that would become the hallmark of Capital One – namely its "information-based strategy" (IBS), which used a database-marketing approach to bring customized solutions to customers. Along with fellow SPA consultant, Nigel Morris, Fairbank persuaded Signet Bank to implement the strategy in 1988. By 1994, the bank's credit card business was growing so fast that Signet spun off Capital One Financial Corporation, making Fairbank CEO, and chairman in 1995.

More recently Fairbank has tried to reduce the company's reliance on credit cards with the purchase of Hibernia National Bank and North Fork Bank, allowing, Capital One to compete with larger financial institutions. He has since raised $750 million from a stock offering and, in a further move towards diversification, bought Chevy Chase Bank in a $520 million merger.

Best Decision:

Developing and using Capital One's "information-based strategy" to customize financial solutions for customers.

Business Lessons:

Keep at it – Fairbank has had to overcome suspicion and resistance to his ideas, but his persistance has enabled him to build a Fortune 500 company from scratch.

Shantanu Narayen

CEO,

Adobe Systems

The software industry was at a crucial stage in its development when Narayen took over as CEO of Adobe at the end of 2007. The emergence of so-called "web 2.0" was in full swing, and the industry's heavy hitters were positioning themselves to maximize their opportunities in this new world of user-generated content, social networks and "rich internet applications". Focusing on software that blurs the boundaries between the web, the PC and the phone, Narayen is ensuring a leading role for Adobe in this new web world.

Biography:

Born in Hyderabad, India, in 1964. He wanted to be a journalist, but his parents insisted, he study electrical engineering at Osmania University in Hyderabad. He moved to the US in 1984 and received a master's degree in computer science from Bowling Green State University, Ohio. He also had a master's degree in business administration from the Haas School of Business Berkeley, California.

Ahead of His Time:

An engineer at heart, Narayen began working in Silicon Valley in the mid 1980s, with spells at Apple and Silicon Graphics, before using $10 million to found Pictra, a digital-image-sharing company. His initiative turned out to be ahead of its time, and he tried to sell the company to Adobe in the late 1990s. Adobe's then-CEO, Bruce Chizen, decided not to buy, but instead hired Narayen as a senior vice president in product research. Narayen's technological insight and strategic vision soon made him a vital part of the leadership team.

Preparing for the New World:

While officially still in charge of only engineering, Narayen was involved in key strategic initiatives. In 2002, concerned about the strength of business sales groups at the company's main competitors, he suggested that Adobe commission more new products. The management agreed, and software sales rose by 42 per cent the following year, underlining Narayen's importance as a behind-the-scenes influence.

Appointed president and chief operating officer at the end of 2005, he initiated the biggest acquisition in Adobe's history, when it paid $3.4 billion for Macromedia, bringing the ubiquitous Flash software into its product portfolio, expanding the company's software platform, and strengthening itts presence in key markets.

As CEO, Narayen has oven seen the launch of Adobe's "next big thing", AIR (Adobe Integrated Runtime), a platform for running web-based applications on a desktop PC, an essential part of his planned expansion into online services and mobile computing.

Leadership Style:

Low-key and cerebral. Narayen has a deep understanding of his field that can cut through prevailing business wisdom and carry people with him.

Business Lessons:

No matter how popular a product has been in the past, a business should not rely on this success to continue into the future. There will always be someone coming up with new products to compete with your current offerings. A business must continue to innovate if it is to thrive in the long term.

- Ask your customers about products. This will help to fine-tune existing products and to develop new ones.
- Instruct innovation teams to be creative. Don't cramp their style with false assumptions of what is possible.
- Talk to your team about what will make customers stop buying your products.

Key Strength:

An intimate understanding of the possibilities of technology and a rare ability to see where it will go.

Best Decision:

Buying Macromedia, which left Adobe ideally placed for the new web environment.

Steve Jobs

Co-founder, Chairman and CEO, Apple

The Archetypal business maverick, Steve Jobs was the face of Apple, the creative force behind its success, and a formidable team builder. He is chairman, CEO, and co-founder of the company (with Steve Wozniak in 1976), founder of Pixar animation studio, and since Pixar's sale to Disney, Disney's largest individual shareholder with an important foothold in Hollywood. Jobs can claim joint authorship of three of the most significant technologies of the past three decades:

1. The Personal Computer (PC)
2. The Graphical User Interface (GUI)
3. Digital music

Biography:

Born in 1955 in San Francisco, Steve Jobs is the adopted son of Paul and Clara Jobs. His biological parents were Joanne Carole Schieble and Abdulfattah Jandali, the latter a graduate student from Syria who became a political science professor. Jobs failed to graduate from his literature, poetry and physics course at Oregon's Reed College. He died of respiratory arrest related to his metastatic tumor on Oct 5, 2011.

Hiring and Firing Up:

One of the keys to Jobs enduring success has been his skill in hiring the best team and firing them up. As a young Apple chairman Steve Jobs boldly stole the then-president of PepsiCo, John Sculley, to be his chief executive. Yet Jobs autocratic style has also caused him problems. Fed up with his unwillingness to be a team player, in 1985 the other Apple directors kicked him out. Aged 30, Jobs was out of a job.

An i for the Future:

Using the proceeds from the sale of his Apple stocks, Jobs soon broadened the scope of his business interests with an adroit acquisition, purchasing the computer graphics division of Lucasfilms (later Pixar) which gave him a key future foothold in entertainment concept. He returned to lead an ailing Apple in 1997.

In the next decade the company's share price rose 36-fold, thanks largely to the success of the iPod and iTunes. From the iPhone to MacBook Air, Apple products ooze desirability and continue to define geek chic. Colleagues describe Jobs as brilliant and a great motivator, but he pushes his team to their limits, and some employees have quit shortly after finishing a product.

Steve Jobs vision and relentless eye for detail have given Apple the kind of brand power other CEOs dream of. He has an unerring ability to create instantly desirable, "must have" products. He starts by asking his team "what do we want?" rather than "what can we produce?". Hardware and software are then invented to produce the dream. Products that fail to excite Steve Jobs himself are dropped or started again from scratch. Apple's strategy focuses on very few products, but these few have become irresistible bestsellers.

Leadership Style:

- Visionary, creative and entrepreneurial.
- Some say an autocratic micro-manager.
- He can be charming and engaging, but some have complained about his indelicate language.

Business Lessons:

Steve Jobs drive, passion and creative imagination permeate the work environment at Apple, and allow him to devolve work in his team. His biographer Leander Kahney has called this phenomenon the "routinization" of charisma. Think of it as branding the team with your own values.

- Brand yourself within – and outside of – the company, and articulate your value to others.
- Do what you love, and integrate your passions with your job tasks.
- Identify supporters and create a network of relationships that support your personal brand.

Key Strength:

He has an instinctive understanding not only of where technology is going but also what makes people want to buy it.

Best Decision:

Developing both the software and hardware elements in the iPod and iTunes combination.

Lessons from Steve Jobs:

- Innovation distinguishes between a leader and a follower.
- Be a yardstick of quality. Some people aren't used to an environment where excellence is expected.
- The only way to do great work is to love what you do. If you haven't found it yet, keep looking. Don't settle. As with all matters of the heart, you'll know when you find it.
- You know, we don't grow most of the food we eat. We wear clothes other people make. We speak a language that other people developed. We use a mathematics that other people evolved... I mean, we're constantly taking things. It's a wonderful, ecstatic feeling to create something that puts it back in the pool of human experience and knowledge.

- There's a phrase in Buddhism, 'Beginner's mind.' It's wonderful to have a beginner's mind.
- We think basically you watch television to turn your brain off, and you work on your computer when you want to turn your brain on.
- I'm the only person I know that's lost a quarter of a billion dollars in one year.... It's very character-building.
- I would trade all of my technology for an afternoon with Socrates.
- We're here to put a dent in the universe. Otherwise why else even be here?
- Your time is limited, so don't waste it living someone else's life. Don't be trapped by dogma – which is living with the results of other people's thinking. Don't let the noise of other's opinions drown out your own inner voice. And most important, have the courage to follow your heart and intuition. They somehow already know what you truly want to become. Everything else is secondary.

Steven Ballmer

CEO,
Microsoft Corp.

With Fanatical Loyalty and a ruthless management style, Ballmer has commanded the largest software company in the world to record profits since being named Microsoft's CEO in 2000.

Biography:

Born in the suburbs of Detroit in 1956. Ballmer graduated from Harvard University with a bachelor's degree in mathematics and economics.

Ballmer has worked for Microsoft since becoming its twenty-fourth employee in 1980. A friend of Bill Gates from University, Ballmer headed up several major divisions of Microsoft, including operations, sales and support, before taking over the reins of the company in 2000. A year later, Microsoft released its popular Xbox gaming console. In 2006, Microsoft announced its largest ever corporate dividend, paying out $32 billion to shareholders. Ballmer has himself made billions as shareholder, and his estimated net worth is $15 billion.

While his years of loyalty to Microsoft no doubt paved the way to his leadership position, so did his competitive and monopolistic instincts. Known for his passionate outbursts, after losing a top engineer to Google, Ballmer is reported to have thrown a chair across a room and sworn he would "****** bury Google". This kind of intense competitiveness may just be what Microsoft needs as Google and Apple continue to grow and Microsoft finds its market share shrinking.

Best Decision:

Introducing the Xbox and moving Microsoft into the popular console gaming industry.

Business Lessons:

All businesses, especially software companies, are like sharks – either you keep moving forwards or you die.

Sunil Mittal

Chairman and CEO,
Bharti Airtel

A self-made man with an eye for a market and an innate business sense, Mittal has created on of the India's most successful company from scratch. From small beginnings, he has brought modern telecommunications system to millions of communication-hungry Indians at prices they can afford, and built a business with a market capitalization that has topped $23 billion, a turnover of $5billion, and more than 50 million customers. Now Mittal is looking to revolutionize the retail sector and the way India goes shopping.

Biography:

Born in India's northern state of Punjab in 1957. Sunil was educated at Punjab University in Chandigarh, India.

Wheeler Dealing:

After graduating, Mittal borrowed $1,500 from his father and set up a bicycle parts business in Ludhiana in his native Punjab. Aware of its limited potential, he moved to Delhi in the 1980s and spotting a potential market, started selling imported generators, with profit margins of up to 100 per cent. As the Indian government began to lift trading restrictions in 1991, Mittal moved into the nascent telecommunications market, supplying handsets. In the 1990s, he moved quickly to capitalize on the new mobile phone market in India, in conjunction with the French telecom group Vivendi.

Calculated Expansion:

In 1983, Mittal became the first person to introduce the push-button handset phone in India. Even affluent Indians had to wait years to have a phone connection installed by state-run providers and Mittal spotted a huge potential market for the private supplier. In the mid-1990s, Bharti Airtel, the company he set up, had fewer than 120,000 subscribers, but the next few years saw a period of enormous growth. His strategy was to offer consumers the best technology with the lowest prices.

Mittal gained a reputation as a man who could attract funding and alliances; both SingTel and Vodafone have been his partners. Mittal believes the next big chance to hit India will be in the retail sector, as shopping habits move away from markets and corner shops into modern air-conditioned supermarkets. The potential worth of the retail sector in India is estimated to be around $200 billion a year. To this end, in 2006 Mittal signed a deal with Wal-Mart to open a chain of stores under the name of BestPrice Modern Wholesale.

Leadership Style:

Passionate and ambitious, Mittal is a great delegator, believing the fastest route to a successful company is allowing staff to show initiative and take decisions.

Business Lessons:

Mittal build his empire through partnerships with a range of overseas companies. While rivals diversified into steel, hotels and aviation, Bharti Airtel linked up with Vivendi to capture the mobile telecoms market. When growth slowed, he applied the same partnership approach to a new area with great potential – the retail sector.

- From partnerships with other suppliers; encourage growth through mutually profitable joint ventures.
- When a partnership has worked well in one market, exploit your people's skills in another.

- Include your managers in partnerships and rely on them to deliver in their own particular way.

Key Strength:

Understanding the needs of the enormous but complex Indian telecommunications market and tailoring products accordingly.

Best Decision:

Attracting millions of new customers by introducing a range of pre-paid mobile phone cards available through India's millions of independent, non-chain, local "mom and pop" stores.

Terry Tai-ming Gou

Founder and CEO,
Hon Hai Precision

Publicity-shy he may be, but Taiwanese businessman Gou cannot hide from the world's media. As founder and CEO of Hon Hai Precision, Gou is the leader of the world's largest contractor of electronics, making products for household names such as Apple, Nintendo and Mortorola. No one has done more to attract electronics production to the Far East, and his company is one of China's key exporters. A notable philanthropist, Gou plans to give away a third of his estimated $5.5 billion personal fortune to charitable causes.

Biography:

Born in Taiwan in 1950.

From Knobs to i-Pods:

Gou's road to riches began in 1974 when his mother loaned him the money to start making channel-changing knobs for televisions. By the early 1980s, the business was doing well enough for him to break into the PC market by supplying connectors. Improved relations between Taiwan and China encouraged Gou to set up his first factory in the city of Shenzhan, China, in 1988.

Keen to expand, Gou travelled throughout Japan and the US in the 1980s and the 1900s, soliciting new customers. It was a meeting in China with Michael Dell, founder of Dell, Inc. that gave a huge boost to his business, and today Hon Hai is one of Dell's biggest suppliers.

By 2000, company revenue had reached $3 billion and Hon Hai's workforce topped 30,000. Gou has since expanded his product lines to include mobile phones, flat-panel LCD monitors, digital cameras and i-Pods, earning a reputation for good quality products at a competitive price.

Building an Empire:

Expansion into China has increased the Shenzhan plant's workforce almost ten-fold, and nearly half a million workers can be found on sites across the mainland. Gou has also extended operations globally, opening new plants in Europe, Central and South America, and all over Asia.

Now too large for Gou to manage alone, Hon Hai still has a very personality-centred management ethos, with large photos of Gou on display and biographies for sale in every plant. Famous for cursing around his sites late at night in his golf cart to check on production and tend to repairs, Gou often works 16 hour days to keep production output successfully on schedule.

Leadership Style:

Charismatic and autocratic, he leads by example. Taking a leaf out of Mao's Little Red Book, Gou has issued a number of "Gou's Quotations", which managers are expected to learn by rote.

Business Lessons:

Gou demands a lot and is somewhat autocratic in style. Though he is sometimes likened to a "medieval warland" in the manner in which he runs Hon Hai, he never asks more than he himself is willing to give.

- Be prepared to lead by example and, like Gou, work long days if necessary to keep customer satisfaction levels high.
- Make an autocratic style work when you need to meet a short-term problem or a long-term strategy.

• Lace autocratic style with charismatic leadership. The aim is to motivate, not to frighten or rule by fear.

Key Strength:

Running Hon hai in the style of a personal fiefdom, Gou is said to inspire great loyalty among his employees.

Best Decision:

Opening a factory in mainland China, where labour cost were more competitive.

Walt Disney

Founder and CEO,
The Walt Disney Company

Known worldwide for his timeless popular creations as an animator, Disney was also a dogged entrepreneur who created a huge and enduring business empire from scratch. As well as facing the usual concerns of any entrepreneur, Disney had to contend with economic depression, world war, unscrupulous competitors, and ever-changing public tastes. His ability to innovate and his determination to keep his sights on his business goals ensured that his company prospered, and it remains a powerful corporate presence.

Biography:

Born in 1901 in Chicago, Disney and his family settled in Kansas City in 1911 when he was nine. He began drawing for his school newspaper and as a driver with the Red Cross during World War I he decorated his ambulance with cartoons. Died in 1966.

False Starts:

When Disney's first studio providing cartoons to local theatres in Kansas City went bankrupt, the determined young entrepreneur moved to Hollywood to try his chances in the movie industry. He had success with a series called Oswald the Lucky Rabbit and hired a team of animators, but when he discovered that he didn't own the rights, nearly all his animators jumped ship, leaving his business in tatters again.

Breaking the Ground:

Undeterred by two business failures, Disney began work on a new character based on a mouse he had kept as a pet while working in Kansas. Mickey Mouse proved to be an immediate hit, as did a number of other creations, and Disney's studio took off, giving him the confidence to begin work on another innovative idea – the first animated feature-length film in English.

After three years, he ran out of money and had to take a rough cut of the film to his bank in the hope of securing further funding. When it was finally released in 1938, Snow White and the Seven Dwarfs became the most successful movie of the year, rewarding Disney's innovation and persistence in creating a whole new genre.

During World War II, labour strikes and the need to produce government propaganda film sent the business into another decline, but it recovered enough after the war for Disney to begin work on a theme park, another groundbreaking concept that was widely derided. The opening of Disneyland and the continuing success of the studio finally set Disney's business on a solid footing, providing the base for the diversification that has built today's media giant.

Leadership Style:

- Disney understood the importance of letting other people's creativity flourish for the benefit of the overall project.
- Sometimes notoriously tough on his employees.

Business Lessons:

Every time he looked like he was on the road to success, Disney took a hit. But every time he learned the lesson, picked himself up and came back stronger, proving that genuine innovators are never finished until they allow themselves to be.

- Take risks, even as a middle manager or team leader. Get a reputation for trying new things.

• Don't allow the entrepreneurial spirit to exist only at the top – look for innovation from everywhere.

• At the end of every event or project discuss and record what went well and what needed improvement.

Key Strength:

Immense determination and an intuitive understanding of what would entertain families.

Best Decision:

Pushing on with *Snow White and the Seven Drawfs*, even though a feature-length animated film had never been made before and he was running out of money.

William McKnight

President and Chairman, 3M

The Minnesota Mining and Manufacturing Company was a struggling young enterprise on the verge of bankruptcy when McKnight became general manager in 1914. By the time he retired as chairman in 1966, 3M was a vast conglomerate with operations all over the world and products that were familiar household names to hundreds of millions of consumers. At the heart of this growth was McKnight's talent for encouraging innovation, the influence of which can be seen in modern management practice.

Biography:

Born in 1887 in White, South Dakota. His parents owned a farm claimed under the Homestead Act, which encouraged the settlement of undeveloped land. He attended Duluth Business University in Minnesota.

The Edge of Bankruptcy:

McKnight joined the business that later became known as 3M as an assistant bookkeeper in 1907, when the company, founded only five years earlier, was struggling to recover from a series of initial blunders that nearly sank it. These errors, including misidentifying a crucial mineral deposit, looked likely to make the enterprise a short-lived one, but McKnight's ability turned 3M around and put it on the path to growth.

Freedom to Innovate:

McKnight quickly recognized that making mistakes was an intrinsic part of innovation and that innovation was the key to success. Putting this insight into practice, he made research the heart of 3M's activities, establishing a laboratory. The research and development approach created breakthrough product after breakthrough product, many of which have remained in use ever since, among them waterproof sandpaper, masking tape, cellophane tape, scotchgard, reflective sheets for highway markings and Post-It Notes.

McKnight also understood that invention required a looser approach to management that allowed people to follow their ideas through. That meant delegating and allowing employees a far greater degree of autonomy than was standard at the time. He allowed his engineers to spend 15 per cent of their time on projects of their own, stimulating creativity.

McKnight formulated a series of pioneering management principles based around the importance of delegation and the idea that, although mistakes will be made, they will be less damaging than the mistakes management will make in telling everyone what to do.

Leadership Style:

Soft spoken but also direct and efficient. McKnight provided strong encouragement and motivation to his employees through his delegating style.

Business Lessons:

Rather than treating them as tools to transmit your directions, trust your people and give them the room to exercise their creativity, even if it means they make mistakes that you could have avoided.

- Record successes and mistakes and make this information accessible to everyone. That way the organization learns from its mistakes.

- Encourage people to look at potential risks, estimating the impact and probability of the risk occurring.
- People are your greatest asset. Make sure that how you look after your people is consistent with your words.

Key strength:

Giving his people free rein to develop their creativity.

Best Decision:

Setting up a small laboratory in 1916, ensuring that 3M's future was guided by science.

Lessons from William McKnight:

- As our business grows, it becomes increasingly necessary to delegate responsibility and to encourage men and women to exercise their initiative. This requires considerable tolerance. Those men and women to whom we delegate authority and responsibility, if they are good people, are going to want to do their jobs in their own way.
- Mistakes will be made. But if a person is essentially right, the mistakes he or she makes are not as serious in the long run as the mistakes management will make if it undertakes to tell those in authority exactly how they must do their jobs.
- Management that is destructively critical when mistakes are made kills initiative. And it's essential that we have many people with initiative if we are to continue to grow.